how to stay way cool!

when things are tough
(and really like it)

Spending Prime
Time With God

how to stay way cool!

when things are tough
(and really like it)

Susan Nally

Broadman & Holman Publishers

Nashville, Tennessee

Acknowledgments

▼

Thanks!

With gratitude to Missy and Kristen for your patience, love,
encouragement, understanding, and helpful ideas
during the writing of this book. Thanks for being there.

Much love to the children of Crievewood Baptist Church
for all you have taught me.
Special thanks to Josh and Amanda for your extra help.

With grateful appreciation to Henry Campbell for his interest,
help, and encouragement during the writing of this book.

Love and thanks to Doug for your support
during the months of writing this book.

Contents

Introduction

▼

How do you stay cool when things are tough? What does it mean to stay cool? Does it mean cold? Does it mean to stay calm or not get easily excited? Does it mean popular? Is someone awesome or considered first-rate if he or she is cool?

What do you mean when you use the word *cool?*

_____

_____

_____

_____

_____

_____

_____

_____

This book will guide you to think about times *you* need to be cool. You see, being the most popular person won't help you *stay cool* in *tough* situations. As you work through this book, you will discover that God can help you stay cool at all times. Learning to rely on God will help you through tough situations. In fact, you might even learn to enjoy some of these tough times.

The following phrases will guide your study:

Tough Times:
a closer look at the Bible passage

Staying Cool:
modern day story or application

Good News:
a verse to learn

Quiet Time:
a prayer or place to write a prayer

Remember, you may work as fast or as slow as you like. Your goal is to have a daily quiet time. Keep your Bible, a pencil, and a highlighter near to use each day.

Prayer is a very important part of each session; please know that God wants you to use this time to communicate with Him. Take a few minutes to write a prayer asking God to guide you through this book._____

_____

_____

_____

_____

Chapter One

Responsibility

▼

Warning! This chapter could be life-changing.

Find the story of Noah and the ark in Genesis 6:8–9:17. Place a marker there so you can find it again easily.

In the word search on the next page, find the following twenty-one words that tell about Noah and being a responsible person. Use a highlighter to mark each word.

chores	responsible	flood
friends	ark	rainbow
promises	family	Genesis
dependable	reliable	assignments
Noah	boring	duty
responsibility	commitment	burden
trusted	obligation	school

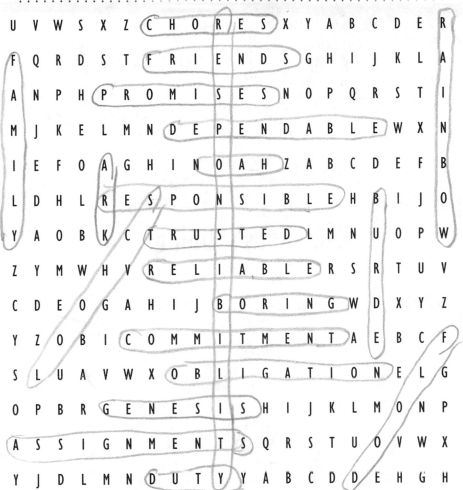

U V W S X Z C H O R E S X Y A B C D E R
F Q R D S T F R I E N D S G H I J K L A
A N P H P R O M I S E S N O P Q R S T I
M J K E L M N D E P E N D A B L E W X N
I E F O A G H I N O A H Z A B C D E F B
L D H L R E S P O N S I B L E H B I J O
Y A O B K C T R U S T E D L M N U O P W
Z Y M W H V R E L I A B L E R S R T U V
C D E O G A H I J B O R I N G W D X Y Z
Y Z O B I C O M M I T M E N T A E B C F
S L U A V W X O B L I G A T I O N E L G
O P B R G E N E S I S H I J K L M O N P
A S S I G N M E N T S Q R S T U O V W X
Y J D L M N D U T Y Y A B C D D E H G H

Chapter's Challenge:

To learn to handle responsibility.

Noah had no faults and was the only good man of his time. He lived in fellowship with God, but everyone else was evil in God's sight and violence had spread everywhere. God looked at the world and saw that it was evil for the people were all living evil lives.
— Genesis 6:10–12

Everybody's Doing It?

▼

Tough Times:
Place a check by the facts you already know about Noah.
_____ 1. Noah was five hundred years old.
__✓__ 2. Noah had three sons.
__✓__ 3. Noah was the only good man around.
__✓__ 4. Noah loved God.
__✓__ 5. Noah lived with corruption.
__✓__ 6. Noah was a model citizen.
__✓__ 7. Noah was close to God.
Now read Genesis 6:8–12 to find out more about Noah's life.

These were definitely "tough times" in which to live. Noah was unquestionably an example of what was right and good. Unfortunately, no one else was. They especially weren't interested in being close to God. Go back and read Genesis 6:1–7 to discover why God needed Noah's help. Why did God think Noah would act responsibly? _____

_____

_____

Staying Cool:

Think about the things going on around you that God would consider evil. Look at the list below. In the space provided write how God could use you to make a difference.

1. guns in school

_____

_____

2. drugs and alcohol

_____

_____

3. "bad" language

_____

_____

4. entertainment choices (movies/videos)

_____

_____

5. treating people badly

_____

_____

Good News:

"Happy are those who reject the advice of evil men, who do not follow the example of sinners or join those who have no use for God" (Psalm 1:1).

Quiet Time:

Lord, please help me remember that "my example" is an important witness for You. Help me act responsibly.

"Build a boat for yourself out of good timber; make rooms in it and cover it with tar inside and out. Make it 450 feet long, 75 feet wide and 45 feet high. Make a roof for the boat and leave a space of 18 inches between the roof and the sides. Build it with three decks and put a door in the side."
— Genesis 6:14–16

Master Plan

▼

Tough Times:

Read again God's instructions for building this boat. Would you agree that they were exact? God knew what He wanted. He told Noah exactly what to do. All Noah had to do was obey.

Open your Bible to Genesis 6:13–22.

God told Noah that he was going to destroy all _____ because of their _____ deeds. In verse 17 God told Noah that he would send a _____ to destroy every _____. Everything on earth would _____, but God promised to make a _____ (agreement) with Noah. After the boat was built God told Noah to take his _____, _____ and their _____ inside the boat. Noah was also instructed to take a _____ and _____ of every kind of _____ and _____ along with all kinds of _____ for all of them. Verse 22 says Noah did _____ that God _____.

For Noah to complete the project he had to pay attention to every detail in the "master's plan." How does being exact show you are a responsible person? _____

_____

_____

Staying Cool:

Amanda and Josh wanted a dog. There were several drawbacks; no fenced-in backyard, community's leash law, no dog house, and working parents.

Dad suggested a family meeting to discuss these roadblocks. He asked Amanda and Josh to come up with a plan to remove the hindrances. "I know I can count on both of you." Their dad continued, "We'll talk tomorrow night and look at your plans."

Pretend you are Amanda and Josh. Use the space below to write plans that will help you get the dog. State your exact instructions and how to carry them out. Remember, for your plans to succeed you must do *everything* exactly as you plan.

YOUR PLANS:

_____

_____

_____

_____

Good News:

"Happy are those who obey his commands, who always do what is right" (Psalm 106:3).

Quiet Time:

Lord, help me to understand the importance of following instructions even though the task seems impossible. With You all things are possible.

"Seven days from now I am going to send rain that will fall for forty days and nights in order to destroy all the living beings that I have made."
— Genesis 7:4

Warning Sign

▼

Tough Times:
Read Genesis 7:1–5 and think about the following statements. Tell how you think the people might have responded.

1. Noah put his whole family on a boat that was sitting on dry land.

_____

_____

2. Noah put seven pairs of each ritually clean animal and bird, and one pair of each kind of unclean animal and bird on this boat.

_____

_____

3. Noah's family and all the animals sat on this boat for seven days while nothing happening.

_____

_____

Noah's boat building caused a lot of excitement in town. This was a time when the people did not know God. Noah's boat was a warning of the coming judgment.

Noah was teased and ridiculed for obeying God. In his day the evil that existed was so great that the people were blind to what God was saying. Nothing stopped Noah from obeying.

Sometimes responsible actions can put you in difficult situations. How can you react responsibly? _____

_____

_____

Staying Cool:

Think about what is happening in your life that could be a warning sign. Do you ever find yourself in difficult situations? Do you ever hope your parents won't find out about something you said or did? Maybe these are warnings. Use the space below like a journal. Tell about those situations. Also tell how you regard the warnings. In other words, what are you willing to do that will show you understand these warnings?

_____

_____

_____

_____

_____

Good News:

"Teach me, Lord, what you want me to do, and lead me along a safe path" (Psalm 27:11).

Quiet Time:

Lord, sometimes it's hard to follow You. Help me to remember You are always there to protect me.

Seven days later the flood came. . . . and rain fell on the earth for forty days and nights. . . . the water became deep enough for the boat to float. . . . water did not start going down for a hundred and fifty days.
— Genesis 7:10,12,17,24

Rockin' & Rollin'
▼

Tough Times:
Think about living conditions on the boat. The smells must have been strong. Think about the crowded conditions. How did Noah's family spend their time?

Read Genesis 7:6 to 8:14 to find clues about life on the boat for over 250 days.

Clue #1: (verse 7:6) Noah's age at time of flood _____
Clue #2: (verse 7:7) people inside boat _____
Clue #3: (verse 7:8) what else went inside _____
Clue #4: (verse 7:10) how long they waited _____
Clue #5: (verse 7:11) describe flood _____
Clue #6: (verse 7:12) how long it rained _____
Clue #7: (verse 7:16) who shut the door _____
Clue #8: (verse 7:20) depth of water _____
Clue #9: (verse 7:23) who survived _____
Clue #10: (verse 7:24) water went down after _____
Clue #11: (verse 8:7) didn't return _____
Clue #12: (verse 8:11) dove returned with _____

Close your eyes; try to imagine the sounds, smells, and feelings of those on the boat.

Staying Cool:

Jeremy's family was leaving on a three week vacation. The entire family worked together to plan the trip. All agreed on what they would see and where they would stop.

The first stop, the Grand Canyon, took two and a half days of driving. Jeremy was tired of sitting in the back of the van. He was tired of listening to his brother and sister argue. He needed to stretch his legs and get some air. He was hungry. He was ready for a break.

Jeremy listened as his mom reminded them of the things they had planned to do at this stop. "I sure am glad we're going to be here more than one day," Jeremy moaned.

Use this space to tell about the sights, sounds, smells, and feelings. What was life like for Jeremy and his family on this trip? For what was Jeremy responsible?

_____

_____

_____

_____

_____

_____

_____

Good News:

"May your constant love be with us, Lord, as we put our hope in you" (Psalm 33:22).

Quiet Time:

Lord, it's hard sometimes to be happy about the situations I find myself in, even though I might have planned them. Help me learn to enjoy.

Noah built an altar to the LORD; he took one of each kind of ritually clean animal and bird, and burned them whole as a sacrifice on the altar.
— Genesis 8:20

Gratitude

▼

Tough Times:

For the first time in more than 250 days, Noah, his family, and all the animals and birds that were with him, left the boat. It must have been a wonderful moment. Look at Genesis 8:20 to discover the first thing Noah did. _____

_____

Was Noah thanking God? (A sacrifice is a ceremony of offering something to God as an act of worship.)

Notice the passage says he used the ritually clean animals and birds. He offered only the *best* to God.

Now look at verses 21–22. Because the "odor from the sacrifice pleased God," He made a promise to Noah. Write the promise found in verse 21–22 in your own words. _____

_____

Noah did something that was very important. He took time to show his gratitude to God for being saved from the judgment. What responsible action did Noah take? _____

_____

Staying Cool:

In your "busyness," many times you forget to say thank you. Think about the difference saying thank you made in the story. Noah not only said thank you, he showed his appreciation by bringing God the best that he had.

Use the rest of this space to express your gratitude to God. What can you bring as an offering that would show your gratitude? Write your thank-you note to God below.

Dear God, _____

_____

_____

_____

_____

_____

_____

_____

_____

_____

_____

_____

_____

Good News:

"Give thanks to the Lord, because he is good; his love is eternal!" (Psalm 107:1)

Quiet Time:

Lord, may I always show my thanks by giving my best to You.

"With these words I make my covenant with you: I promise that never again will all living beings be destroyed by a flood; never again will a flood destroy the earth. As a sign of this everlasting covenant . . . I am putting my bow in the clouds."
— Genesis 9:11–13

The Promise

▼

Tough Times:

Noah received a promise from God. Look closely at the covenant (agreement) God made with Noah. Read Genesis 9:8–17. How many times did you find the word *covenant?* _____ God wanted to make sure that Noah understood the importance of this covenant. What sign did God place in the sky for this everlasting covenant? _____

God's promise to Noah was not only for Noah. It is for everyone.

Read verses 12–17 again. Close your eyes. Remember the last time you saw a rainbow. What did it look like? How did you respond? Did you think about God's promise?

To share your feelings about God's promise, draw a rainbow on a separate sheet of paper and then write words across the rainbow that describe the rainbow and what it means to you.

Staying Cool:

A covenant is an agreement between two or more people. A promise is a pledge that one will or will not do something.

You make covenants/promises all the time. Sometimes you keep them and sometimes you don't. Do you agree?

Make three lists of your covenants/promises. List the covenants/promises you've made related to family, school, and God.

FAMILY	SCHOOL	GOD
_____	_____	_____
_____	_____	_____
_____	_____	_____
_____	_____	_____
_____	_____	_____
_____	_____	_____

Highlight covenants/promises that you've kept. Now look at the others on your lists. What caused you to break them? What could you have done differently? _____

_____

_____

_____

_____

_____

If a covenant/promise is worth making, it is worth keeping! You should make them carefully!

Good News:

"Come, let us praise the Lord! Let us sing for joy to God, who protects us!" (Psalm 95:1)

Quiet Time:

Thank You, Lord, for the rainbow and its promise. It reminds me of Your faithfulness.

Noah did everything that God commanded.
— Genesis 6:22

How Am I Responsible?

▼

Tough Times:
Turn back to the word search in the introduction to this chapter. Find the four words that describe a responsible person. Write them.

D_____   T_____

R_____   C_____

Think about how these words described Noah. Noah was definitely dependable. Tell how. _____

_____

Noah proved he could be trusted. Why could God trust Noah?

_____

_____

List the things that Noah did that proved he was worthy of God's trust:

_____

_____

The word *reliable* means that you can be counted on to do what you say. How does that word describe Noah? _____

_____

_____

The last word you should have listed is *commitment.* It takes commitment to finish what you start. Why was it important for Noah to be committed to this project? _____

_____

_____

Staying Cool:
Tell how the four words—*dependable, trusted, reliable,* and *commitment*—describe you as a responsible person. Then share what you wrote with a parent. See if he or she agrees. If you're having trouble with this, spend a few minutes talking to God, then try again.

_____

_____

_____

_____

_____

_____

Good News:
"Indeed he did great things for us, how happy we were!"
(Psalm 126:3)

Quiet Time:
God, You have done great things for me. Help me to learn from Noah and act responsibly.

Chapter Two

Fighting

▼

Fight: to battle; struggle against; quarrel; argue; try to overcome; a contest; to stand up against; assert oneself; to try to prevent or undo; to defend against or drive back.

In this chapter you will think about what happens when you fight. Read again all the definitions printed above. Do you fight in any of these ways?

The following questions will guide your study:
- Why do you fight?
- What do you fight about?
- With whom do you fight?
- How do you fight?
- Where do you fight?
- When do fights happen?

Each session deals with a reason for fighting. When you finish the chapter, you will have identified six different reasons (causes) for fighting. Each day you will be asked to tell what the fighting accomplished (results).

Throughout the Bible you learn that God wants His people to live in peace with one another. Many things happen every day that keep you from experiencing that peace.

Chapter's Challenge:
Learn to live in peace.

"If you had done the right thing, you would be smiling; but because you have done evil, sin is crouching at your door. It wants to rule you, but you must overcome it."
— Genesis 4:7

Jealousy and Envy

▼

Tough Times:

Today's passage is the story of Cain and Abel. Turn in your Bible to the first book of the Old Testament. Read Genesis 4:1–12, a story about two brothers.

Match the character traits in the center column with the correct brother's name on either side.

	TRAITS	
	Oldest	
	Victim	
	Shepherd	
	Killer	
CAIN	Jealous	ABEL
	Gave Best	
	Younger	
	Farmer	
	Punished	
	Favored	

Jealous means being resentful toward someone who has more than you do.

Envy means not being happy about someone else's good fortune and wanting that same good fortune yourself. What happened in this story because of jealousy and envy? _____

_____

_____

Staying Cool:

Think about the last time you were jealous or envied someone. What happened because of those feelings? Did those feelings cause you to fight?

Use the space below to tell your story by answering the *who, what, where, when, why,* and *how* about the situation. In your story include what you will do differently next time. Share your story with someone. _____

_____

_____

_____

_____

_____

_____

Good News:

"I gain wisdom from your laws, and so I hate all bad conduct" (Psalm 119:104).

Quiet Time:

Lord, it's really hard to admit I want something that belongs to someone else so much that I would do something to harm them or cause them to lose out. Forgive me.

He [Moses] went out to visit his people, the Hebrews, and he saw how they were forced to do hard labor. He even saw an Egyptian kill a Hebrew.
— Exodus 2:11

Anger
▼

T o u g h   T i m e s :
Find Moses' story in Exodus 2:11–15 and read it.
Important facts about Moses:
- found by Pharaoh's daughter in basket at side of river
- raised as Egyptian prince in Pharaoh's palace
- well educated
- never forgot his people
- different
- somebody special
- hot tempered
- hasty
- ready to take a stand for what he thought was right

Moses got angry when he saw the Egyptian beat the Hebrew. Then Moses tried to hide what he did as a result of his anger. Who knew about the murder? _____
Was it all right for Moses to feel angry? Was the behavior caused by the anger right or wrong? Moses ran away and hid to save himself from Pharaoh.

Anger is a strong feeling toward someone who opposes, insults, or hurts; a feeling of extreme displeasure; rage; wrath.

Moses' anger got the best of him. Does anger ever get the best of you? What part does anger play in your life? How do you react when you are angry? _____

_____

_____

Staying Cool:

Read the story. Write an ending that shows the results of anger.

Doug and Brad were having fun in the best snow of the year. They had been playing outside all day.

Even though they were tired they didn't want to go inside just yet. "Hey Doug, let's sit on this wall and throw snow balls at passing cars." Doug looked a little surprised, but decided to play along. He didn't want to spoil their fun.

"I guess that's all right, but we better be ready to run," Doug said. Brad laughed, "You really don't think someone would stop, get out of their car, and come after us." Both boys laughed as they made their snowballs.

Traffic was moving slow. The streets were a slippery mess. After missing several cars both boys landed snowballs right in the center of the windshield of the next car. The car skidded out of control. When the car stopped, its front wheels were on the sidewalk in front of the boys.

A man slowly got out of the damaged car. He was furious. He . . .

_____

_____

Good News:

"Don't give into . . . anger; it only leads to trouble" (Psalm 37:8).

Quiet Time:

Lord, sometimes I let my anger control me. Forgive me. Help me remember anger hurts and destroys.

When his brothers saw that their father loved Joseph more than he loved them, they hated their brother so much that they would not speak to him in a friendly manner.
— Genesis 37:4

Left Out/Lies/Slighted

▼

Tough Times:
Read Genesis 37 to understand what life was like in this family. Review the facts listed under each name.

JOSEPH	BROTHERS	JACOB
youthful dreamer	shepherds	father
favorite son	liars	old man
handsome, spoiled	hurt	son of Isaac
tattler	hated Joseph	showed favoritism
insensitive	sold Joseph	gave fancy coat

When it came to getting along, this family really had some big problems. Eleven of Jacob's sons found themselves feeling "left out" because their father showed more love to their brother Joseph.

These feelings led to unkind words and hatred. They even caused the brothers to lie to their father after they got rid of Joseph. The lies told about Joseph's death caused sorrow and grief.

Think about your family. Do you ever feel left out or slighted?

What happens when you let those feelings take control? Answer those questions after you read the following story.

Staying Cool:

"I'm gonna tell!" "You're in trouble!" Joey ran off yelling and laughing in a sing-song voice.

Christy watched with daggers darting from her eyes. "He thinks he's so smart. I wish he'd learn to mind his own business."

Trouble was always brewing between Christy and Joey. They were always fighting about something. It was becoming really hard to know whom to believe. Most of the time Christy got in trouble just because she was the oldest. She never understood that. Joey was always telling half truths. Sometimes he even made things sound worse than they were.

Most of the time Christy tried to stay out of his way. She rarely talked to him. They never played together. She felt she always came out on the short end with her parents where Joey was concerned.

Have you ever felt like Christy? _____ Tell about those feelings.

_____

_____

What happens when those feelings take control of you? _____

_____

Share your feelings with someone you think will understand.

Good News:

"Teach us how short life is, so that we may become wise" (Psalm 90:12).

Quiet Time:

Lord, I don't like being left out. I know that when I feel that way I don't make the best decisions about how to act. Please help me understand my feelings.

Goliath stood and shouted at the Israelites, "What are you doing there, lined up for battle? I am a Philistine, you slaves of Saul! . . . I dare you to pick someone to fight me!"
— 1 Samuel 17:8,10

Big Mouth/Bully!

▼

Tough Times:
The story of David and Goliath is familiar. You probably already know that young David killed the giant, Goliath, with a slingshot and stone. Look closely at the things Goliath said.

Turn to 1 Samuel 17. Read verses 4–16. Describe Goliath.

_____

Tell what you learned about David from verses 12–15. _____

_____

Verse 16 tells that Goliath challenged the Israelites every _____ and _____ for _____ days.

Read verses 41–44, then make a list of what Goliath said to David that showed he was a "big mouth" and a "bully." _____

_____

_____

How does someone's big mouth affect you? Do you ignore it? Are you bullied by their words to do things you might not otherwise do? A *bully* is a person who acts tough and likes to fight people who are smaller or weaker. A bully also likes to frighten others into doing things.

Staying Cool:

The bus ride home every day seemed to last forever. Each day Erin tried to sit close to the front, but many times she found herself too near the back of the bus and Adam.

Adam thought he was so cool. He found all kinds of ways to make Erin's life miserable. One day he teased her about her new high top tennis shoes. Another time he knocked her books under the bus. Then he loudly exclaimed how clumsy she was. His big mouth seemed to never miss an opportunity to give her a hard time.

Erin was always embarrassed. She tried hard to ignore Adam. The longer it went on the madder Erin got. Finally she'd had enough. Finish the story by telling what you would do. Include the results of your actions. _____

_____

_____

_____

_____

_____

_____

Good News:

"I will be careful about what I do and will not let my tongue make me sin" (Psalm 39:1).

Quiet Time:

Forgive me, Lord, when I use my mouth in unkind ways. I don't like others to bully me; help me to not pick on others.

"So this is how you act! I swear that I won't stop until I pay you back!"
He attacked them fiercely and killed many of them.
— Judges 15:7

Revenge/Pay Back

▼

T o u g h   T i m e s :

Revenge is bringing injury or harm to someone as punishment or to pay back for a wrong. Today you will look at Samson, the Hebrew folk hero. He got revenge because he was very angry over a family matter.

Turn in your Bible to Judges 13–16. Samson was known for his great physical strength. Many thought he was unbeatable. They believed that Samson's strength came from his long hair, but it came from God.

Even though Samson was strong, he had some weaknesses. Read through the list of his character traits:
- headstrong
- strong
- little or no self-control
- courageous
- played with temptation
- acted alone
- childish

Highlight the character traits that you consider weaknesses.

Many of these traits led Samson to seek revenge. More than once in these four chapters you will discover that Samson paid the Philistines back for something he considered a wrong. To read all of this interesting story, read Judges 13–16.

Do you ever want revenge? Think about the times that you have said, "I'll get you for that." Did you mean it? What did you do?

_____

_____

Staying Cool:

Ask a parent to help you finish this session. Find a story in your newspaper that shows someone taking revenge for a wrong they thought they had suffered. Discuss the story with your parent.

In the space below briefly give the details of the story and then tell the result of the revenge. _____

_____

_____

_____

Who was hurt the most? _____

_____

_____

If you don't have a newspaper, write your own story.

Good News:

"Turn away from evil and do good; strive for peace with all your heart" (Psalm 34:14).

Quiet Time:

Dear God, help me to remember that revenge does not make me happy. It only separates me more from others and from You.

"Your brother came and deceived me. He has taken away your bless-ing."
— Genesis 27:35

Rejection/Deceit

▼

T o u g h   T i m e s :
The story of Esau and Jacob found in Genesis 27 is one of rejection and deceit. *Deceit* is the act of lying, cheating, or misleading anoth-er. *Rejection* is the act of refusing to accept or to deny something.

Esau, the older twin, should have received certain rights and privileges. Esau was denied what was rightfully his when his brother lied to their father. Jacob, with the help of his mother, deceived his father and cheated his brother Easu. Read the story in Genesis 27.

Jacob's deception took some hard work because these twin brothers were very different. Jacob made his brother so angry that Esau wanted to kill him.

God planned for families to live together happily. God does not want children to lie and cheat. When families live in an atmosphere like Easu and Jacob, bad things happen. Tell what bad things hap-pened in this story. _____

_____

_____

Have you ever been denied something because someone was deceived? Share the incident and how you reacted. _____

_____

_____

Staying Cool:

Paul's dad had recently remarried. The new wife had two kids—a girl, Lucy, and a boy, Larry. Every other weekend they all were together. Paul had to share his room. This was a problem.

Last weekend when Paul arrived for his visit, his dad told him they needed to talk alone in the den. "Sure, Dad. What's up?"

Paul's father didn't look happy. "Are these yours? Larry found these magazines under the mattress."

Paul didn't like this. "No, sir. I've never seen those before."

For a few minutes Paul and his dad were silent. Then Dad again asked about the magazines. Paul was surprised. "Don't you believe me, Dad? Has someone said they are mine?"

"I'm afraid that we have a problem," Dad continued. "Larry says they are yours. Who do I believe?"

"Well, you better believe me!" Paul jumped up, furious. "Why would I want those magazines? They're garbage and so is Larry."

What do you think will happen next because of this incident? Did Larry deliberately deceive Paul's dad? Does Paul have a right to be angry? Finish the story._____

_____

_____

Good News:

"Save me, Lord, from liars and deceivers" (Psalm 120:2).

Quiet Time:

It's hard to get along with people that try to get me in trouble. Forgive me when I lose control and get angry.

"We are relatives, and your men and my men shouldn't be quarreling. So let's separate. Choose any part of the land you want. You go one way, and I'll go the other."
— Genesis 13:8—9

Peacemakers

▼

T o u g h   T i m e s :

Read Genesis 13:1–13 to discover how Abraham acted as a peacemaker. If peace is living in harmony, then a peacemaker is someone who works to settle disputes. A peacemaker is willing to compromise.

Abraham and Lot had been traveling together for a long time with all of their possessions. The group with them was very large. In verses 1–5 find who and what was in the group. _____

_____

_____

Verse 6 tells why they were quarreling. _____

Read verse 7 to find out who quarreled. _____

What did Abraham say to Lot in verses 8–9 that lets you know he wanted peace?_____

_____

_____

Verses 10–11 tell how the quarrels were resolved. _____
_____

Do you think it was easy for Abraham to compromise? Is it easy for you to compromise so that you can live in peace with your family and friends? _____
_____

Staying Cool:

Write a story that tells how you or someone you know was a peace-maker. Remember to include what happened because of the will-ingness to compromise. _____
_____
_____
_____
_____
_____
_____
_____
_____

Good News:

"How wonderful it is, how pleasant, for God's people to live together in harmony!" (Psalm 133:1)

Quiet Time:

Help me, Lord, to learn to be willing to compromise so that I can be a peacemaker.

Chapter Three

Hard Tests

▼

What did you think of when you saw this chapter title? Did you only think about tests at school?

You experience "hard tests" all the time. Every choice you make might be considered a test. Some choices are harder than others. Think about the last difficult choice you made. Why was it a difficult choice (hard test)? Did you make the right choice? How do you know?

Open your Bible to the Old Testament book of Jonah. God commanded the prophet Jonah to do something. Jonah found himself facing hard tests because of what God asked him to do. Read Jonah's story in this short book and learn how Jonah responded to these hard tests. It will challenge you to look at how you might respond to hard tests you face.

Find the verses listed. Tell about God's request of Jonah and how the prophet responded. (Use the clues in parentheses.)

Jonah 1:1–2 _____

_____(God's command)

Jonah 1:10 _____

_____(wrong)

Jonah 1:12 _____

_____(blame)

Jonah 1:17 _____

_____(punishment)

Jonah 2:1–10 _____

_____(forgiveness)

Jonah 3:1–2 _____

_____(obeyed God)

Jonah 3:4 _____

_____(command)

Jonah 3:10 _____

_____(change)

Jonah 4:1 _____

_____(God's goodness)

Chapter's Challenge:

To know how to stay way cool when faced with a hard test.

*"[God] said, "Go to Nineveh, that great city, and speak out against it;
I am aware of how wicked its people are." Jonah, however, set out in
the opposite direction in order to get away from the LORD.*
— Jonah 1:2–3

Disobedience

▼

Tough Times:

God asked Jonah to go to the city of Nineveh to tell the people of
His love. God did not like their lying, stealing, cheating, and
killing. God wanted them to change their ways.

The mission was to go to the hometown of his enemies. Jonah
was afraid to tell them to change the way they lived. He could be
hurt or killed.

Have you ever been asked to go and do something you didn't
want to do? This was definitely a "hard test." God was expecting a
lot from Jonah. God expects a lot of you.

Jonah had a choice. He could obey God and go to Nineveh.
Our Scripture tells us he chose to run away in the opposite direction. Jonah thought he could go where God couldn't find him. He
hurried off to catch a ship to a far away land.

Did God expect Jonah to do something he couldn't do? Was
the test too hard? When Jonah chose to disobey God, did he fail
this test? Wrong choices like Jonah's often lead to even
tougher choices.

Staying Cool:

Think of Jonah's command from God as being sent on a "special mission." The mission was to go tell his enemies to change the way they lived.

In this session you will start a story. You will send yourself on a "special mission." You will have a difficult message to deliver. Remember God is commanding you to go. Fill in the appropriate information below, then tell how you responded when you received your command. Remember, this is only the beginning of your story.

Time or Year: _____

_____

Place being sent: _____

_____

People involved: _____

_____

Message: _____

_____

Start your story: _____

_____

_____

_____

_____

Good News:

"Teach me, Lord, what you want me to do, and lead me along a safe path, because I have many enemies" (Psalm 27:11).

Quiet Time:

Dear Lord, help me to be obedient even when obeying You will be a hard test. Help me find the courage to obey.

"That was an awful thing to do! The storm was getting worse all the time, so the sailors asked him, "What should we do to you to stop the storm?" Jonah answered, "Throw me into the sea, and it will calm down. I know it is my fault that you are caught in this violent storm."
— Jonah 1:10–12

Wrongdoings

▼

Tough Times:

At the end of session one, Jonah was boarding a boat. The boat pulled away and Jonah began to relax. He decided to lay down in the bottom of the boat. It wasn't long before the boat was being tossed about by strong winds from a bad storm. The sailors tried hard to control the boat. They threw their supplies and things overboard to lighten their load. Fear overcame the sailors. They cried out to their gods for help. Everything looked hopeless.

Jonah was found asleep. The crew questioned Jonah. Jonah was courageous. He told them he was running away from God. This made the sailors fear Jonah's God.

The sailors didn't want to die at sea. They asked Jonah what they should do to stop the storm. What did Jonah tell them?

_____

This passage presents two tough situations. Name them.

_____and

_____

First, the storm could have killed everyone on the boat. Second, the sailors' fear of Jonah's God made them wonder if they should throw Jonah overboard as he suggested.

Staying Cool:

Continue telling the story you started in session one. Review what you have already written. Think about what happened to Jonah in this part of the Bible passage. Your story today should cover what happened because you disobeyed. Do not solve the problem; only tell what happened. Leave your story incomplete to start again in your next session.

"The Mission Continues"

_____

_____

_____

_____

_____

_____

_____

Good News:

"God is our shelter and strength, always ready to help in times of trouble" (Psalm 46:1).

Quiet Time:

Dear Lord, help me to have the courage to admit when I have made a wrong choice. Help me to be willing to solve the problem that I helped create.

Then they picked up Jonah and threw him into the sea, and it calmed down at once. This made the sailors so afraid of the LORD that they offered a sacrifice and promised to serve him. At the LORD'S command a large fish swallowed Jonah, and he was inside the fish for three days and three nights.
— Jonah 1:15–17

Danger or God Finds Jonah

▼

Tough Times:

Jonah gave the sailors a solution to their problem, but they were reluctant to follow his suggestion. The sailors tried to get the ship to safety. The storm grew stronger. They were in great danger.

Then the sailors called out to Jonah's God in a prayer. They asked the Lord not to punish them for throwing Jonah into the sea and causing his death.

Close your eyes and picture the scene. Describe what you see.

_____

_____

_____

Jonah was thrown overboard. The Bible passage tells us the seas "calmed at once." This should have made the sailors happy, but they were more afraid. They offered a sacrifice to the Lord and promised to serve Him. Jonah's willingness to sacrifice his life to save them was a powerful witness.

Jonah was not lost to the sea. God sent a large fish to rescue

Jonah. How long did Jonah stay inside the fish? _____

_____

Do you think Jonah was surprised by what happened? _____

Staying Cool:

Jonah's disobedience put people's lives in danger.

Think about the direction your story is taking. Have your choices put lives in danger? Are your decisions a witness for God?

In this part of your story you find yourself facing the results of your actions. Tell what will happen.

"The Mission Continues"

_____

_____

_____

_____

_____

_____

_____

_____

Good News:

"When I am afraid, O Lord Almighty, I put my trust in you" (Psalm 56:3).

Quiet Time:

Dear Lord, thank You for this story about how You are willing to use people even when they disappoint You. Lord, use me to be a witness for You so that others may know You.

"In my distress, O LORD, I called to you and you answered me. From deep in the world of the dead I cried for help, and you heard me."
— Jonah 2:2

Seeks Forgiveness

▼

Tough Times:
Open your Bible to Jonah 2:1–10 and read Jonah's prayer. Jonah was in a strange place to pray. Where was he?

_____

The first thing Jonah did was let God know he was thankful for His help. He recognized God's goodness (verse 2).

Jonah drew an unforgettable word picture of what had happened to him. Read again verses 3–7. Could you feel the "waters all around" and the "mighty waves rolling over" Jonah? Then he told about the "sea covering him completely" and the "seaweed wrapping around his head." What a hopeless feeling Jonah must have had. In verse 6 Jonah said he "went down to the very roots of the mountains." By that he meant the bottom of the sea.

What did Jonah say in verse 7 to let you know that he thought he was dying? _____

_____

In verses 8–9, Jonah once again offered praise and thanks to the one true God. He said he would offer a sacrifice and do all that he had promised. In this prayer Jonah revealed his personal relationship with God.

Jonah's circumstances did not keep him from praying. Even Jonah the sinner could call on God and ask for help and forgiveness.

In the last verse in chapter 2, what was the Lord's order to the fish? _____

_____

Staying Cool:

Your story today will be your prayer to the one true God. Model your prayer after Jonah's prayer. Make it a prayer of thanksgiving and praise to God for His goodness to you. Remember this prayer should show what kind of relationship you have with God. You may want to reread Jonah's prayer.

YOUR PRAYER:

_____

_____

_____

_____

_____

_____

Good News:

"Remember that the Lord has chosen the righteous for his own, and he hears me when I call to him" (Psalm 4:3).

Quiet Time:

Take the next few minutes to reread your prayer. Then sit quietly and think about what you wrote.

Once again the LORD *spoke to Jonah. He said, "Go to Nineveh, that great city, and proclaim to the people the message I have given you." So Jonah obeyed the* LORD *and went to Nineveh, a city so large that it took three days to walk through it.*
— Jonah 3:1–3

Because Jonah Obeys

▼

Tough Times:

A second time God spoke to Jonah. Had anything changed? God was still asking Jonah to do the same thing. This time Jonah, the messenger, had a different attitude. Jonah obeyed God. He went to the "great city" of Nineveh.

Jonah went to Nineveh to deliver the message. Look at verse 4 in your Bible to discover the message. Write the message.

_____

_____

Remember from an earlier session you learned that the people of Nineveh were the enemy. They were a lying, stealing, cheating, and killing group of ungodly people.

Jonah walked through the city telling everyone what would happen if they did not change. The people listened to Jonah. They knew he was a great prophet that was speaking for God.

After the people heard they told the king. Everyone, including the king, put on _____ and sat in ashes. This was their way of showing that they were sorry for the way they had been living. The people also went without food (fasted) and prayed for forgiveness.

Do you think the people's actions surprised Jonah? Jonah, the prophet and messenger, was used by God to call these people to repent (turn away from) their sins.

Staying Cool:

When the people listened, things started happening. In your story today, once again tell about the place you are being sent and the message you are to deliver. Unlike the first time, though, you obey the command. Be sure to tell how you feel about what happens.

"The Mission Continues"

_____

_____

_____

_____

_____

_____

_____

_____

_____

_____

Good News:

"Trust in the Lord and do good; live in the land and be safe" (Psalm 37:3).

Quiet Time:

Lord, it feels good when I obey. Thank You for those good feelings. Help me to follow all of Your commands for my life. Help me remember those good feelings next time I think about disobeying You.

God saw what they did; he saw that they had given up their wicked behavior. So he changed his mind and did not punish them as he had said he would.
— Jonah 3:10

Change of Heart

▼

Tough Times:

Wait a minute. Didn't God say he was going to destroy Nineveh in forty days because of their wickedness? Why did God change his mind?

In the last session you discovered that the people believed the message and prayed for forgiveness. To show that they really wanted to change they did three things. List them.

1. _____

2. _____

3. _____

You probably learned as a young child that God is a God of love. God listened to the prayer of repentance from the people of Nineveh. He showed his love for them by not destroying the city.

Jonah was then faced with a problem. God didn't do what Jonah had said. Jonah must have wondered, *Will the people laugh at*

(fasted)
(sat in ashes)
(put on sackcloth)

me? Will they listen to me the next time? Jonah was sure the people would think he was not a good prophet.

Jonah should not have been surprised, especially since God had forgiven him when he disobeyed. God listened to Jonah's prayer; why wouldn't He listen to the people of Nineveh's prayer?

Think about these questions: Did Jonah deserve forgiveness more than the people of Nineveh? Did Jonah have a right to be upset? How were the people of Nineveh feeling about God's "change of heart?"

Staying Cool:

In His goodness, God chose to accept the people of Nineveh's appeal for forgiveness. As you write your story today, remember to include God's goodness. Think about what you have learned from Jonah as you conclude your story today.

"The Mission Concludes"

_____

_____

_____

_____

_____

_____

_____

Good News:

"You are good to us and forgiving, full of constant love for all who pray to you" (Psalm 86:5).

Quiet Times:

Thank You, God, for forgiving me when I sin. Help me to remember that You are also as forgiving of others.

Jonah was very unhappy about this and became angry. So he prayed, "LORD didn't I say before I left home that this is just what you would do? That's why I did my best to run away to Spain! I knew that you are a loving and merciful God, always patient, always kind, and always ready to change your mind and not punish"... The LORD answered, "What right do you have to be angry?"
— Jonah 4:1–2, 4

Jonah Learns

▼

Tough Times:
Review the list of Jonah's "hard tests":

1. Jonah disobeyed God's command
2. Jonah ran away to hide from God
3. Jonah put lives in danger
4. Jonah was thrown overboard to calm the storm
5. Jonah was swallowed by a large fish
6. Jonah pleaded with God
7. Jonah was spit out on the beach
8. Jonah obeyed and delivered God's message
9. The people listened and asked for God's forgiveness
10. God changed His mind

How did Jonah act when God did just what Jonah thought He would do? Jonah _____

_____

Are you ever like Jonah? Do you want others to be punished differently? Is it all right for you to do wrong, then ask and receive forgiveness, but not all right for others to do the same?

God treats everyone the same!

Staying Cool:

What does this mean in respect to how you treat others? The last time you did wrong did you ask for and receive forgiveness? Do you want God to offer the same forgiveness to others?

In the space below share what you have learned about staying cool when you face the following hard tests.

1. Obeying

_____

_____

2. Admitting wrongdoings

_____

_____

3. Needing forgiveness

_____

_____

4. Being angry

_____

_____

5. Feeling disappointed

_____

_____

Good News:

"Praise the Lord, my soul, and do not forget how kind he is. He forgives all my sins" (Psalm 103:2–3).

Quiet Time:

Help me, Lord, know how to stay cool when faced with hard tests.

Chapter Four

The Race Is On!

▼

Preparations for your "race":

Mental:

First—"Shake off" old ideas or expectations about what you will learn and how well you will do.

Second—"Imagine" the race.

Third—"Sit quietly." Ask God's help in completing the race.

Physical:

First—"Warm up" that cold muscle (your brain).

Second—"Get ready" for the start.

Many of life's most important lessons are learned from competition. Daily you compete for many things. Make a list of ten ways you compete (include more than just sports).

1. _____
2. _____
3. _____
4. _____
5. _____
6. _____
7. _____
8. _____
9. _____
10. _____

In this chapter you will study six different passages that talk about races. The following questions will be your guide:

- What are the expectations for my success?
- Do the best always win?
- What must I do to win?
- What happened to my "superior" ability?
- What happens when I lose?
- How do I keep from selling out?

Chapter's Challenge:
To always be ready to compete.

Like an athlete eager to run a race.
— Psalm 19:5

Expectations for Success

▼

Tough Times:
The Bible passage above comes from a psalm telling about the greatness of God and how the sun was pleasing in God's sight.

This verse is comparing the sun to an athlete that is eager to run a race. Every day the sun starts in the east, travels across the sky, and then sets in the west. Every day the sun runs the same race.

With every race there are expectations. What word is used to describe the athlete? _____

Eagerness needs to be channeled in the right direction. When a runner is too eager he might "jump the gun," causing a false start. His nerves might get the best of him.

Staying Cool:
Pete was excited about his first wrestling tournament. He'd practiced hard. His coach was confident he could compete.

The Saturday of the match Pete woke up early. As Pete lay in his bed he realized he was both excited and scared. This was Pete's first competition. He really wanted to do well.

Pete ate a big breakfast. Then his dad drove him to school. First thing Pete had to do was weigh in. Pete could start his warm-ups after he weighed. The longer Pete waited in line, the more nervous he got. *What if I'm over the weight limit?*

Finally it was Pete's turn. Coach noticed Pete was nervous. He walked over beside Pete. "Hey, guy, how's it going?"

Pete tried to smile as he stepped on the scales. Both watched as the scale registered at the exact weight limit. Finally, Pete smiled as he said, "I was really worried about making my weight class."

Coach nodded that he understood. "Next time don't eat breakfast before you weigh. Every ounce counts!"

As Pete warmed up he thought about what the coach said. "I could have really messed things up. I'd have been so embarrassed."

How did Pete show that he was "eager to succeed?" _____

_____

Were Pete's expectations too high? What had Pete done that allowed him to have those high expectations? _____

_____

_____

Should you always expect success? _____

Think about the pressure that expectations put on you. Who else has expectations for you? Do those expectations affect your performance? How? _____

_____

Good News:
"Like an athlete eager to run a race" (Psalm 19:5).

Quiet Time:
Lord, help me to be hopeful about success. Help me to remember that hard work will prepare me for success. Help me to handle other people's expectations so they don't create too much pressure.

I realized another thing, that in this world fast runners do not always win the races, and the brave do not always win the battles. . . . Bad luck happens to everyone."
— Ecclesiastes 9:11

Winning Ways!
▼

Tough Times:
Our Scripture passage says the "fast runners do not always win the race." That doesn't sound fair. Do you agree or disagree? _____
Why? _____

_____

_____

To be the fastest or best runner, you must work hard. Practice until you have it right. Then should you expect to be the winner? That's not what the verse is saying. It's saying just the opposite. Maybe that's why the verse ends with the warning about bad luck.

Staying Cool:
The ice skaters were finishing their second day of competition. Tomorrow night's competition will determine the members of the next Olympic Figure Skating Team. Tensions around the ice rink were high.

Nancy skated off the ice and was preparing to cover her blades when from out of nowhere she was attacked. Something hard was hit across her knee

As she crumbled to the floor she cried out for help. The pain was apparent from the expression on her face. Shock and disbelief surrounded her. "Who could do such a horrible thing? Why would someone want to hurt me?"

Nancy lay in her father's arms crying. Whoever attacked her had disappeared.

The pain was unbelievable, but the fear of not being able to skate was worse. Nancy was lifted onto a stretcher and into a waiting ambulance. The trip to the hospital seemed endless. "What will happen," she wondered. "This just can't be happening!"

The best part of the story is how Nancy handled herself then. She never accused anyone. She waited calmly to see what the Olympic committee would do. She really showed her true character.

Unfortunately the story you just read is true. Nancy Kerrigan, Olympic figure skating hopeful, was attacked. Her injuries did keep her from skating in the finals.

Would you classify this as bad luck? Tell what you think that phrase means: _____

_____

Have you ever been on the receiving end of bad luck? Did you feel like a victim? Tell about your experience and how you reacted.

_____

_____

How you respond will show your winning ways.

Good News:
"He gives me new strength. He guides me in the right paths, as he has promised" (Psalm 23:3).

Quiet Time:
Lord, many times things happen that I don't understand. Many times life doesn't seem fair. Please help me understand and know how to respond.

Surely you know that many runners take part in a race, but only one of them wins the prize. Every athlete in training submits to strict discipline.
— 1 Corinthians 9:24–25

Self-Discipline

▼

Tough Times:

Look at the Bible passage. It reminds you there is always more than one runner in a race. The verses also say only one person wins. The next part of the passage is what is important. Did you know strict discipline is what makes the difference in who wins? Think about what discipline means and in what ways are you disciplined or not disciplined?

Staying Cool:

It's so boring running all these laps, Mark thought. *I just hate it.*

Mark's coach was watching from the center of the field where other team members were completing their workouts. Coach Jones was surprised Mark looked so sluggish. In the last meet Mark had placed second and third in his two races.

When Mark came off the track, Coach walked over for a chat. "All finished?" Mark looked up surprised to be getting the attention. "Yes, sir. It was really hard today."

Coach sat down on the grass to continue the talk while Mark did his cool-down exercises. "You're right, Mark. Some days are harder than others. That's when you have to try harder. Mental toughness is just as important as physical toughness. Maybe you need to work on your self-discipline."

Mark looked up, confused. "What's that got to do with anything?"

Coach smiled. "Self-discipline is what makes you practice. You have to want to do this enough to make yourself do it. Then you will achieve the positive results you want."

Look back at today's story. In your own words tell what you think the coach was trying to explain to Mark.

_____

_____

_____

_____

Think of a time you were in a competition where self-discipline was important. Describe the competition. Then tell the results.

_____

_____

_____

Good News:
"Teach me your ways, O Lord; make them known to me" (Psalm 25:4).

Quiet Time:
Lord, help me to remember that self-discipline is what directs my actions. Help me to practice so I can always do my best no matter what the competition.

You were doing so well! Who made you stop obeying the truth? How did he persuade you?
— Galatians 5:7, GNB

You were running a good race. Who cut in on you and kept you from obeying the truth?
— Galatians 5:7, NIV

Superior Ability

▼

Tough Times:

In the two Bible passages you see the phrase "obeying the truth." It tells us that when we stop obeying the truth we might stop doing well in something. If the truth is found in the Bible, how can *not* obeying the truth make us lose control of a situation?

_____

_____

Staying Cool:

"I am the best! I am the best!" the boxer shouted as he paraded around the ring. He had just put on a superior display of his ability. Tonight he was better than his opponent.

After a few minutes the audience's cheers turned to boos. The boxer stopped, twirled around the ring and glared at the crowd. Someone yelled, "Don't act too cocky. There'll be other fights." Others joined in the jeers.

The boxer let his anger get the best of him. *I'll show them,* he thought. He stomped his feet at the audience and started yelling, "I am the greatest! I am the greatest!"

People started filing out of the arena shaking their heads and mumbling about the boxer being a bad sport. "Too bad the guy lost control," one fellow said to his friend. "He looked pretty awesome during the fight, but his actions after the fight don't make any sense."

Do you ever not use good sense? Respond to these events in the story by telling how the boxer hurt himself.

1. shouting "I am the best!" _____

_____

_____

2. parading around the ring _____

_____

_____

3. getting angry _____

_____

_____

The boxer "blew it!" Tell about a time you lost control of your "good sense" during some kind of competition. Tell the results.

_____

_____

Good News:

"Examine me, O God, and know my mind; test me, and discover my thoughts. Find out if there is any evil in me and guide me in the everlasting way" (Psalm 139:23–24).

Quiet Time:

Forgive me, Lord, when I lose control. Let my ability speak for itself. Don't let me ruin a good performance by losing control.

Do everything without complaining or arguing. . . . You must shine among them like stars lighting up the sky, . . . it will show that my effort and work have not been wasted."
— Philippians 2:14–16, GNB

I did not run or labor for nothing.
— Philippians 2:16, NIV

Shining Star?

▼

Tough Times:
The Bible passages show us that a good attitude and hard work will help us through any hard test or difficult situations. What do you need to work hard on right now? _____

_____

Staying Cool:
Suzie's class was preparing to compete in the district spelling contest. Suzie was one of the best spellers in her class. She knew she was good, but her goal was to be the best.

The class worked hard each week on the fifty assigned words. Each night Suzie worked at home. Weekly practice contests helped Suzie feel more confident. The more she practiced the less nervous she became. Suzie woke up feeling terrible on the day of the contest. After a quick check, Mom said, "Back to bed, young lady, I'm calling the doctor. Is your side still hurting?"

Suzie immediately started arguing, "Please don't, Mom. You don't understand; I've just got to go to school today."

Quickly, Mom stopped Suzie's tantrum. "Suzie, your fever is

too high and your side still hurts. Get back to bed, right now."

"All that hard work for nothing," cried Suzie on the way to the hospital. "Why do things always get messed up? It's just not fair!" Suzie spent the next three days recovering from an appendectomy. Every time someone came to visit she complained. After one visitor left, her mom said, "You're complaining surprises me. I thought you knew better."

Pretend you are watching this story happen. Share how you feel about the following:

1. Suzie's goal to be the best:

_____

2. Suzie's preparation:

_____

3. Suzie getting sick:

_____

4. Suzie's reaction:

_____

5. Suzie's attitude:

_____

6. Mom's response to Suzie's complaining:

_____

Suzie's hard work was not wasted. She did learn a lot from the preparation for the contest. In your journal, tell what Suzie lost. What happens when you argue and complain?

Good News:
"Lord, place a guard at my mouth, a sentry at the door of my lips. Keep me from wanting to do wrong" (Psalm 141:3–4).

Quiet Time:
Too often my disappointment is an excuse for arguing and complaining. Help me, Lord, be more like You.

"Let us run with determination the race that lies before us."
— Hebrews 12:1

Not Selling Out

▼

Tough Times:

The Bible passage today suggests that determination is a key ingredient in the successful completion of any race. What does determination mean to you? _____

_____

How do you show determination? _____

_____

Staying Cool:

An exciting new program was announced in Julie's class. All middle school kids could join the new "Odyssey of the Mind" team. It was a competition using teams to create a solution to a problem. *Sounds interesting,* Julie thought.

Julie and several of her friends attended the first meeting where Mrs. Shaw explained the program. "This is a big responsibility. We'll even need your parents' help."

Each person was given a letter with a permission slip. "Looks like serious business," Julie whispered to her friends. "Let's form our own team."

The teams began to work on their creative solution to the problem. Each week they met after school for two hours. Two weeks before the first competition, the girls began to pull things together. Everything was looking good. Everyone was doing her part. What fun they were having!

The last Saturday of the month was finally here. Julie's team met an hour early to practice their presentation one more time. All props were ready and everyone knew their part. They were determined that nothing would keep them from doing their best.

When the competition was over, Mrs. Shaw congratulated each team as she discussed the judges' suggestions. Girls, I'm especially pleased with your presentation. Each one of you has worked very hard.

Tell what the girls' team did that showed their determination.

_____

_____

Were the girls successful because they were willing to work hard? The story doesn't tell if they won the competition. What in the story lets you know of their success? _____

_____

_____

Being a part of an Odyssey team was a big challenge for the girls. The girls' hard work paid off. What are you a part of that's a big challenge? Have you worked hard and done your part? Are others counting on you?_____

_____

_____

Good News:
"My conduct will be faultless" (Psalm 101:2).

Quiet Time:
Lord, help me to enjoy the challenges I have accepted. Help me to work hard for the success of all I do.

"Let us run with determination the race that lies before us."
— Hebrews 12:1

Rewards of Running

▼

Tough Times:

Sometimes situations we face are like a race. We must be disciplined, work hard, and be determined if we want to get through a situation. Sometimes people refer to life as a race, too. We must follow the same attitude and behavior all our lives to be what God wants us to be.

Staying Cool:

Each day this week you have looked at different Scripture passages that deal with competition. Review by doing the three-way match.

Match titles to Scriptures to characters in each story.

SCRIPTURES	TITLE	CHARACTERS
Psalm 19:5b	Expectations for Success	Boxer
Hebrews 12:1c	Self-Discipline	Suzie
Ecclesiastes 9:11	Shining Star?	Julie
Galatians 5:7	Winning Ways	Pete
1 Corinthians 9:24–25	Not Selling Out	Mark
Philippians 2:15–16	Superior Ability	Nancy

Your challenge for today is to pick the one area of competition that gives you the most trouble. Tell what you have learned that will help you make changes in your attitude and behavior.

_____

_____

_____

_____

Write a plan of action that will help you compete in a competition or situation. Remember these keys: eagerness and expectations, winning ways, discipline, losing control, complaining and arguing, and determination.

_____

_____

_____

_____

_____

_____

_____

_____

Good News:
"God is my helper" (Psalm 54:4).

Quiet Time:
Lord, now that I know where I need help and have made plans to change my attitude and behavior, help me to follow through with my plans.

Chapter Five

Tough Family Times

▼

Is it "tough" to be "cool" when dealing with family situations?

The book of Ruth tells a wonderful story about Naomi and her family. This story deals with disappointment, loss, pain, tragedy, joy, and happiness.

How do you deal with disappointment, loss, tragedy, pain, joy, and happiness? Can these be tough times for your family? Naomi's story shows the importance of faith in all the events you will examine. It is *the* important ingredient you will need when dealing with your "tough family times."

Define *faith:* _____

_____

_____

Tell how your belief in God makes the difference in how you respond to tough family times.

_____

_____

_____

_____

_____

_____

Ask God to help you honestly explore your feelings about your tough family times as you work through this chapter.

Chapter's Challenge:
To learn to act responsibly in tough family times.

Again they started crying. Then Orpah kissed her mother-in-law good-bye and went back home. . . . Naomi said to her, "Ruth, your sister-in-law has gone back to her people. . . . Go back home with her." But Ruth answered, "Don't ask me to leave you!" . . . When Naomi saw that Ruth was determined to go with her, she said nothing more.
— Ruth 1:14–18

On the Move

▼

T o u g h   T i m e s :
What makes moving tough? The following words describe the moving experience. Think about how each word makes you feel.

CHANGE   LEAVING
NEW PLACE   FRIENDS
UNKNOWN   LOSS
FEAR

Find Ruth 1:14–15 in your Bible. Write all the words you can find from this passage that make you think *negatively* about moving (hint: crying). _____

_____

_____

S t a y i n g   C o o l :
Tom and Sue were surprised by the announcement. They never expected their mom to pick up and move back to the old farm.

The conversation immediately started to turn into a shouting match. "Why do you want to go live at that old place? I can't think of anything more depressing," argued Tom.

"Me either," Sue cried. "That old place is just awful. There's nothing there."

It was obvious this was a very unpopular decision. Janie Fry really had a battle on her hands. Tom and Sue weren't cooperating. She decided to let them have some time to think things over.

"Hopefully, you'll be more understanding about our situation when you cool off," said Mrs. Fry sadly. "It's not like we have much of a choice."

Tom and Sue were left sitting in the middle of the floor pouting. As their mom left, she tried to smile, but was obviously disappointed with them.

Tom and Sue are being asked to move. Is their response to the move surprising?_____Why? _____

Why would moving be difficult for you?_____

_____

_____

How could Tom and Sue have made this tough family time easier?

_____

What have you learned from this tough family time? _____

_____

Good News:
"In him I trust, and will not be afraid" (Psalm 56:11).

Quiet Time:
Lord, help me to not let my disappointment result in thoughtless behavior.

"When I left here, I had plenty, but the LORD has brought me back without a thing."
— Ruth 1:21

Life's Losses

▼

Tough Times:

Read Ruth 1:19–22. What had happened to Naomi? _____

_____

How did she feel about her situation? _____

_____

Naomi was returning to her homeland and to her family and friends. Verse 19 tells that the whole town was _____ about her return. In the next verse you discover that Naomi did not share that feeling? She told them not to call her Naomi because her life was _____.

Naomi's life had changed since she left Bethlehem. She was now a widow with no money, home, or way to make a living in her old age. Life was tough and Naomi was not feeling good about it. Did she have a right to be angry? _____

Naomi did have one thing going for her. Verse 22 tells you that _____, the Moabite daughter-in-law, was with her. It also tells that the _____ was just beginning. The tough times caused Naomi to lose.

Staying Cool:

After Tom and Sue cooled off, the family sat down to discuss the move. "I hope you both will be more reasonable now." Janie Fry continued, "Last month there were some changes at work. It has been hard for me to continue working there."

Tom and Sue knew how much their mom liked her job. They were surprised she would consider quitting.

"Kids, I know you are unhappy with my decision. I am sorry, but the loss of my job and other expenses make it necessary for us to move." Mrs. Fry told them she was already considering another job.

Tom and Sue sat speechless for several minutes as they thought about all this. It finally dawned on them; they really were moving.

Mrs. Frye talked again with Tom and Sue about the move. Why was it necessary for them to be reasonable?_____

What was lost and why? _____

What three reasons were given for the move? Has a family loss created tough family times for you?_____

_____

How did you respond? _____

_____

Tell how your response made the situation better or worse._____

_____

Good News:

"May he give you all you desire and make all your plans succeed" (Psalm 20:4).

Quiet Time:

Lord, help me to be open to new ways to solve problems, even when I don't understand why things happen that cause me to lose what I care about.

"In addition, Ruth the Moabite, Mahlon's widow, becomes my wife."
— Ruth 4:10

Life's Celebrations

▼

Tough Times:
Find and read Ruth 4:1–12. Marriage to a widow of an Israelite required certain things. Verses 1–5 tell about some of individuals' rights and customs of that day.

Before Boaz could even consider marriage to Ruth, the closest relative had to be found. Then he had to be offered first chance at buying the field that belonged to Naomi's husband. In that day women were not allowed to own property. With the purchase of the land came the responsibility of the daughter-in-law. If Ruth had any children, they would inherit this land upon the death of this man. Ownership of land was sacred and at all costs stayed within a family.

Where does this story take place? _____

Who offers the land to the relative? _____

Does the relative want the land at first? _____

How does this relative answer Boaz in verse 6? _____

What custom did you learn about in verse 7? _____

Who witnessed the sale in verse 2? _____

Why were witnesses necessary? _____

Many things had to happen before Boaz could marry Ruth. Boaz showed respect for the closest relative's rights, loyalty to God's covenant, and love for Ruth. What joy there must have been at this wedding celebration.

Staying Cool:

Life on the farm was different, but Tom and Sue settled in better than expected. They made some new friends and liked their new school and church.

So far the biggest challenge for the children was living with their grandparents. Janie Fry needed her parents' help because there was no after school program available.

Things were going smoothly until one night Mom announced she had invited someone to dinner. Both the children yelled, "Who?"

Smiling, Mom said, "His name is Jack Price. I met him at last month's church fellowship. I hope you don't mind that I've asked him for Friday night." It sounded harmless, but they would watch carefully.

It took only a few months of dinners, dates, and family outings for Tom and Sue to tell their mother really liked Jack. After a year of dating, the wedding was announced. Everyone was excited, including Tom and Sue.

In this story things are different. Janie Fry and her children have faced the changes in their lives. Not all were welcome changes, but they still faced them together. What new change are they now facing? _____

What can keep this from being a tough family time?

_____

Good News:

"May he be pleased with my song, for my gladness comes from him" (Psalm 104:34).

Quiet Time:

Lord, help me face the changes that come in my life with the love and help of my family.

Elimelech died and Naomi was left alone with her two sons who married Moabite girls. . . . About ten years later Mahlon and Chilion also died, and Naomi was left all alone without husband or sons.
— Ruth 1:3–5

Tragedy
▼

Tough Times:
Read Ruth 1:1–5, then make a list of situations that you consider a tragedy: _____

_____

Naomi and her sons moved from their home in Bethlehem to the foreign country of _____ because of the _____. The first bad thing (tragedy) that happened was her husband _____ died. Verse 3 says Naomi was left alone with her _____, who married Moabite girls. What were the sons' names? _____
Verses 4–5 tell you that about _____ years later the second bad thing (tragedy) happened. Who died this time? _____ Naomi was really left all alone this time.

Naomi was in a foreign country with no family. What could she do? Who could she turn to for help? Even though Naomi had no family left, she did have two daughters-in-law living with her.

Tell about a tragedy that created a tough family time for you.

_____

_____

_____

Staying Cool:

Once again Tom and Sue's family life changed. They lived in another new place with their mom and her new husband.

Tom and Sue still went to their grandparents after school. They enjoyed being on the old farm. It had become a special place for them. Each afternoon Grandma had snacks for them and time to talk.

Early one Sunday morning the children awakened to a ringing phone. Tom and Sue heard their mom crying. Jack called for them to come to the kitchen. Both looked anxiously at their mom. She told them their grandpa died during the night.

Tom ran from the room crying and yelling, "No!" as he threw himself onto his bed. Sue ran into her mother's open arms crying, "How could this happen? He was all right yesterday. I don't understand." Mom tried to comfort Sue while Jack followed Tom to his room. Jack sat quietly on the side of the bed and waited for Tom to stop crying.

When a family has to deal with death, it is a tough time. When you lose someone you love, it is a tragedy and you feel very sad.

Has your family had to deal with death? Who helped you? Who did you help? _____

_____

_____

Share with a parent your feelings about death and dying.

Good News:

"The Lord is my shepherd" (Psalm 23:1).

Quiet Time:

Lord, the pain that I feel when someone dies hurts. Please help the hurt to go away and help me understand.

"So she got ready to leave Moab."
— Ruth 1:6

Leaving Home
▼

Tough Times:

Read Ruth 1:6–14. Leaving home is hard. Naomi had this sad experience twice. First she left Bethlehem as a wife and mother. Then she left her home in Moab and moved back to Bethlehem. Even though she knew she would be better off back with her people, the leaving was hard.

What makes leaving so hard? Leaving always means change. Naomi had to say good-bye to two young women that she cared about and loved. She thought both Ruth and Orpah should stay in their homeland with their parents. Naomi encouraged them to leave her. Read verse 9, then describe the parting. _____

_____

Which daughter-in-law left Naomi? (verse 14) _____
What did the other one do that lets you know she did not leave Naomi? _____
Do you think the leaving was harder on Naomi or Orpah? _____
Why? _____

_____

Was the leaving so painful that Ruth couldn't leave Naomi or was there another reason Ruth couldn't leave her? _____

Naomi was a wonderful friend as well as mother-in-law to Ruth.

Staying Cool:

Life on the old farm had been hard since Grandpa's passing. It just was not the same. Grandma always needed help. There just wasn't enough money to hire all the help needed.

One night at dinner Janie asked Tom and Sue to stay at the table. "You know how hard it has been for Grandma to be out at the farm by herself. You have also heard us talking about what it's costing to keep things going." Janie looked sad as she talked to her children. "Grandma and I decided that she needs to leave the farm."

As the words sunk in, the children's shock and disappointment was evident. "But, Mom, we don't want Grandma to leave!" cried Tom.

"No, we sure don't," Sue agreed. "Where would she go? Where would we stay after school? Who'll take care of us?"

Mom understood their pain. She had thought of those questions too. "That's something we'll have to work out. Right now, we have to think about what's best for your grandmother."

How will Grandma's leaving change things for Tom and Sue?

_____

How will Grandma's leaving change things for grandma?

_____

How would you respond to this tough family time?

_____

Good News:

"Your constant love is my guide; your faithfulness always leads me" (Psalm 26:3).

Quiet Time:

Lord, letting someone you love leave is hard. Help me to know how to respond when someone has to leave.

So Boaz took Ruth home as his wife. The Lord blessed her, and she became pregnant and had a son.
— Ruth 4:13

New Life

▼

Tough Times:

Read Ruth 4:13–17 to find out the rest of the story.

Answer the following questions to discover the important facts.

1. Who had a son? _____

2. Who had a grandson? _____

3. Who named the child? _____

4. What was the child's name? _____

5. What would the child do for Naomi? _____

The birth of this child to Ruth and Boaz brought much joy to everyone. Naomi was now a proud grandmother. She was honored by her family and neighbors.

This new life presented more changes. It was a new beginning. Naomi had suffered disappointment, embarrassment, loss, and anger at all that had happened in her life. For a time she was even bitter, but this baby brought joy and happiness to her life. He also brought security for her old age.

Staying Cool:

When Tom and Sue woke on Saturday morning they noticed their mom wasn't feeling good. She smiled rather sheepishly as Jack put their breakfast on the table. "Good morning, kids."

Tom and Sue knew something wasn't right. But what? Finally, Sue questioned, "Are you sure you shouldn't be in bed? You don't look so great this morning."

"It's nothing serious." Their mom continued, "I'm afraid you might see me like this for several more months."

Mom was almost never sick. What could be the matter? Janie and Jack smiled at each other as they said, "We have some exciting news."

Tom and Sue looked at each other then shouted, "Well, what is it?"

Smiling, Janie looked at both her children and said, "I love you both very much. When you were born you added so much joy to my life. You are the most wonderful things in my life."

The children beamed at their mother. "Hurry! Tell us."

Janie continued, "Tom and Sue, how would you like to have a new baby brother or sister?" The room fell silent. The shocked looks said it all.

What was the news? _____

Why do you think Tom and Sue were shocked? _____

_____

How would you respond to this news? _____

_____

_____

_____

Good News:
"When you give them breath, they are created; you give new life to the earth" (Psalm 104:30).

Quiet Time:
Lord, help me to look to You for guidance when life brings big changes.

"That man is a close relative of ours, one of those responsible for taking care of us."
— Ruth 2:20

Responding to Life's Challenges

▼

Tough Times:

In this chapter you looked at some tough family times. You were challenged to respond to some of those times as if they were happening to you.

Use the six words below to help tell about how you can act responsibly when you have these feelings:

Disappointment: _____

_____

Loss: _____

_____

Happiness: _____

_____

Tragedy: _____

_____

Joy: _____

_____

Pain: _____

_____

Staying Cool:

This week you should have learned that how you respond does make a difference. More often than not, your reaction to changes creates tough family times. Did you figure that out?

Now that you have completed this study, in the space below share what you have learned about how you should care for your family in times of change.

_____

_____

_____

_____

_____

_____

_____

_____

_____

_____

_____

_____

Good News:

"The Lord is good; his love is eternal and his faithfulness lasts forever" (Psalm 100:5).

Quiet Time:

Lord, thank You for helping me better understand my responsibility toward my family. Help me not to make the tough times tougher.

Chapter Six

Measuring Up!

▼

How do you measure your success? What tells you
whether you pass or fail? What influences how you think
about yourself?

Grade yourself honestly on the report card below. Use
the numbers 1 through 5. A "5" means "I consider myself
very successful in this area," and "1" means "I feel very
*un*successful in this area."

PHYSICAL		MENTAL	
weight	_____	school	_____
height	_____	home	_____
looks	_____	church	_____

EMOTIONAL

showing love _____

being kind _____

being gentle _____

being courageous _____

arguing _____

SOCIAL

with friends _____

with family _____

with teachers _____

SPIRITUAL

at home _____

at school _____

at church _____

with friends _____

with family _____

with others _____

UNDERSTANDING

of self _____

of others _____

of God _____

Chapter's Challenge:

To know and accept yourself for who you are and what you can become.

"Test us. . . for ten days," he said. "Give us vegetables to eat and water to drink. Then compare us with the young men who are eating the food of the royal court, and base your decision on how we look."
— Daniel 1:12–13

Special Diet

▼

Tough Times:

Does food play a big part in your life? How concerned are you with what you eat? Open your Bible to Daniel 1. Read verses 8–16 to discover why Daniel didn't want to eat the food from the king's court.

Daniel was a slave in Babylonia and had no say in what he ate. He was chosen for a select group and trained to serve the king. The king wanted Daniel and the others to grow strong. During their three years in training, they were served food from the king's table.

Why did Daniel not want to eat the rich food? (verse 8)_____

_____

What do you think of Daniel's suggestion to the guard in verse 12?

_____

Could you eat only vegetables and water? Why or why not? _____

_____

When the ten days were up (verse 15), how did Daniel look? _____

_____

What did Daniel prove by eating the "special diet"? _____

_____

Daniel's physical condition was measured by the way he looked and his strength. How do you measure your physical condition and strength?

Staying Cool:
Think about what you normally eat during a day. Include snacks, soft drinks, and all junk food you eat between meals. Write your list on the left side. On the right side ask your parent to help you write a diet that will help you be healthier and stronger.

WHAT I EAT IN A DAY   MY SPECIAL DIET

Breakfast: Breakfast:

Lunch: Lunch

Dinner: Dinner:

Snacks: Snacks:

How do the two measure up? Are you willing to make some changes in the way you eat so you will be healthier and stronger?

Good News:
"Keep me from wanting to do wrong" (Psalm 141:4).

Quiet Time:
Lord, help me to know that all foods aren't good for me. Help me have the will power not to eat those things that will keep me from being healthy and strong.

They had to be handsome, intelligent, well-trained, quick to learn, and free from physical defects, so that they would be qualified to serve in the royal court.
— Daniel 1:4

Mental Toughness!

▼

Tough Times:

Today's session has to do with how you use your mind. Open your Bible to Daniel 1. Read verses 1–6, and then list the five requirements to be chosen for this special group:

1. _____   4. _____

2. _____   5. _____

3. _____

Read verses 17–21 to find what God gave the four young men.

_____

Daniel was also given skill in _____

_____

Who impressed the king the most?_____

_____

Daniel and his three friends measured up better than anyone else. No matter what question the king asked or what problem he raised, these four knew ten times more. How did they do it? _____

_____

What would it take for you to do that well? Are you willing to work harder? Are you willing to do your homework *every* night? Will you do extra work? Do you believe you can do better? It all starts with believing you can and then doing what it takes (working hard).

Staying Cool:

Do you think you are smart? Do your grades always reflect how much you know? Do you think grades are a fair way to measure knowledge?

Today, write a letter to yourself. Tell how you really feel about school, grades, and the pressure of "measuring up."

Dear Self,

_____

_____

_____

_____

Share your letter with a parent. Talk about what you wrote. What will change because of what you have learned? _____

_____

Good News:

"Examine me, O God, and know my mind; test me, and discover my thoughts" (Psalm 139:23).

Quiet Time:

Lord, help me believe in my ability to learn and do my best. Help me remember that grades aren't always a fair measure of what I know.

Among those chosen were Daniel, Hananiah, Mishael, and Azariah, all of whom were from the tribe of Judah. The chief official gave them new names.

— Daniel 1:6–7

Relationships

▼

T o u g h   T i m e s :

The relationships a person has tell a lot about him or her. Read Daniel 1:1–7. Who did Daniel find himself with? _____ Does the passage say how long Daniel and these three young men had known each other? _____ You should have discovered they were all from Judah and were probably all taken captive at the same time. They may have been life-long friends.

These four young men's relationship grew because of their circumstances. The connection between Daniel and the others must have grown stronger after three years of eating the same food, studying, and living together.

Read Daniel 1:17–19 to find out what happened at the end of the three years. Together they impressed the king more than any of the others. It was at this time that they were made members of the _____ (verse 19).

No doubt the four young men learned to depend on each other. Daniel seems to have been the leader. Maybe the others were good followers.

Relationships connect people. Families, friends, school, church, and sports activities all bring you into different kinds of relationships. Think about how these relationships affect your life.

Staying Cool:

Since this chapter is about measuring yourself, what do your relationships say about you? Read the question again. In the space below, list the main relationships in your life (parents, sisters, brothers, best friends) on the left. On the right, list the positive things each relationship says about you.

Relationship   What It Says About You

_____   _____

_____   _____

_____   _____

_____   _____

_____   _____

_____   _____

_____   _____

Look at your list. Are these relationships that need help because you don't have anything positive to say? Think about how you might change that.

Good News:

"Happy are those who reject the advice of evil men, who do not follow the example of sinners or join those who have no use for God" (Psalm 1:1).

Quiet Time:

Lord, help me choose wisely the people with whom I develop relationships. I know that they will affect my life.

At that the king flew into a rage and ordered the three men to be brought before him.
— Daniel 3:13

Then Nebuchadnezzar lost his temper, and his face turned red with anger at Shadrach, Meshach, and Abednego.
— Daniel 3:19

Cool in the Fire

▼

Tough Times:

Today's Bible story is an exciting and almost unbelievable account of a time when Daniel's three friends chose to obey God. Read Daniel 3:8–25 to find out what happened.

Why were the three friends in trouble? (verse 12) _____

_____

What did the king do when he heard of their disobedience? (verse 13)

_____

When the king gave the men a chance to defend themselves, how did they respond? _____

_____

As you read the passage, did you notice the emotions of the main characters? Describe how the three friends reacted to the king's order to throw them in the fiery furnace (verses 16–18).

_____

_____

_____

Describe how King Nebuchadnezzar handled the situation (verse 19).

_____

Who exercised the most control over their actions and reactions?

_____

What did the three friends learn about their faith in God? _____

_____

What did the king learn from this experience? _____

_____

Staying Cool:

Who or what controls your actions or reactions? You are faced with many tough situations every day. Will you measure up to your tough situations like the three friends or will you be more like the king and lose your cool? Tell about a tough time.

Situation: _____

_____

What made it tough? _____

_____

What actions did you take? Did you react in a good or bad way?

_____

What did you learn from the situation? _____

_____

What will you do differently the next time? _____

_____

Where do you get help in knowing how to respond?_____

_____

Good News:

"My conduct will be faultless" (Psalm 101:2).

Quiet Time:

Lord, may my behavior always show that You are in control of my life.

"I praise you and honor you, God of my ancestors. You have given me wisdom and strength; you have answered my prayer and shown us what to tell the king."
— Daniel 2:23

Gifts

▼

Tough Times:
Daniel and his friends had been through three years of training for the king's court. Read again Daniel 1:17–21. Daniel and his friends had remained faithful to God during their training. Verse 17 tells that God gave them _____.
What special gift did God give Daniel? _____
     Read Daniel 2:17–19. Daniel's gift of interpreting dreams saved his life and his friends' lives. What did Daniel do that lets you know he relied on God (verse 18)? _____
Daniel offered another prayer to God in verses 20–23. This is a prayer of thanks. In verse 20 Daniel said God is _____
and _____. In verse 21 he said God controls _____
and the _____. He _____ and _____
kings. God gives _____ and _____.
     In verse 22 Daniel said that God reveals things that are _____
and _____. The next part of the verse talks about darkness and light. Where did Daniel say God is?_____
The last verse of the prayer lets you know Daniel's true feeling about God. He gave God thanks for his gifts of wisdom and strength. Daniel acknowledged God had answered his prayer by

telling him what the king's dream meant.

Would you say Daniel and his friends depended on God? What difference did God make in the lives of Daniel and his friends?

Staying Cool:

God has given you certain gifts (talents and abilities). Have you thanked Him? Write a prayer of thanksgiving for what God has done for you. Model your prayer after the prayer in Daniel 2:20–23. Tell Him in your prayer what difference He makes in your life.

_____

_____

_____

_____

_____

_____

_____

_____

_____

_____

_____

_____

Good News:

"Let us come before him with thanksgiving and sing joyful songs of praise" (Psalm 95:2).

Quiet Time:

Thank You, God, for all the gifts that You have given me. Help me to use them wisely.

There, just as he had always done, he knelt down at the open windows and prayed to God three times a day.
— Daniel 6:10

Courage

▼

Tough Times:
Read Daniel 6:1–10 to find out why kneeling and praying at an open window was an act of courage. What was the order issued by the king (verse 7)?_____

_____

Why was the order issued (verses 3–5)?_____

_____

What was the punishment for disobeying the order (verse 7)?_____

_____

Did Daniel know about the order when he knelt down to pray at the open window (verse 10)?_____

Read the rest of the story in Daniel 6:11–23. Who was the most upset at Daniel being caught? (verses 14–16) _____
What does the king say in verse 16 about Daniel's God? _____

_____

Who saved Daniel's life?

_____

Verse 22 says that God sent an _____ to shut the mouths of the _____. Why did God save Daniel? _____

_____

Verse 23 says that when Daniel was pulled from the pit unharmed, it was because he trusted God.

List the three ways that Daniel showed courage in this story.

1. _____

2. _____

3. _____

Staying Cool:

On the "Graffiti Wall" below are words that are ways one can show courage. Highlight or circle all the words that describe your courage.

DEPEND ON SOMEONE   stand up for someone   bravery
caring   not fighting
do the right thing   doing your BEST   trusting or trust
peacemaker   FAITH
compromise   BELIEVE in someone   OBEYING RULES

Why did Daniel have courage? _____

_____

What will it take for you to be courageous like Daniel?_____

_____

Good News:

"Be strong, be courageous, all you that hope in the Lord" (Psalm 31:24).

Quiet Time:

Many times it's hard to be courageous. Help me to rely on Your strength to do and say the right things.

"Daniel, don't be afraid. God has heard your prayers ever since the first day you decided to humble yourself in order to gain understanding."
— Daniel 10:12

Understanding

▼

Tough Times:

Over and over in the book of Daniel you read about Daniel interpreting dreams. Do you have to be smart or have some kind of special ability to interpret dreams? Remember Daniel 1:17 says that God gave Daniel the skill to interpret visions and dreams.

Read Daniel 10:1–14 to find the vision Daniel was having. Three different times in this passage the word *understand* or *understanding* is used. What was the vision about that Daniel was trying to understand? _____

_____

The key to understanding is found in verse 12. Why did Daniel have the ability to understand? _____

_____

What does it mean to humble yourself? The word *humble* means "not proud." A humble person is someone that is modest and does not think he is better than others. Daniel totally depended on God. He did not think he was more important than anyone else.

Total dependence on God brought Daniel the gift of understanding. Does that mean that Daniel just sat around and was lazy?

I don't think so. Daniel studied hard, learned, did his job well and had strong friendships. How would you say Daniel measured up?

Staying Cool:

Measure Daniel's success using the 1 to 5 scale.

PHYSICAL

height _____
weight _____
looks _____

MENTAL

school _____
home _____
church _____

EMOTIONAL

showing love _____
being kind _____
being gentle _____
being courageous _____
arguing _____

SOCIAL

with friends _____
with family _____
with teachers _____

SPIRITUAL

at home _____
at school _____
at church _____
with friends _____
with family _____
with others _____

UNDERSTANDING

of self _____
of others _____
of God _____

Review your grades in the introduction to this chapter. Do you now have a better understanding of how to measure yourself? Go back and regrade yourself by giving yourself a second grade to the right of the first grade.

Good News:

"Give me understanding, so that I may know your teachings" (Psalm 119:125).

Quiet Time:

Lord, help me to grade myself fairly.

Chapter Seven

Words! Words! Words!

▼

Words are a group of sounds that have meaning and form our language. As a baby your first word may have been "mommy" or "daddy." Today you speak and understand many more words than you could count. How you use words is what this chapter is all about.

Make a list of ten good and bad ways you use words. Give an example of each. This may take a few minutes. Don't be in a hurry.

TOP TEN

1. _____   6. _____
2. _____   7. _____
3. _____   8. _____
4. _____   9. _____
5. _____   10. _____

In this chapter you will look at several Old Testament verses that tell about using words to gossip, lie, curse, flatter, argue, and to be a busybody. In the last session you will have the opportunity to compare your list of "Top Ten" uses with what you have learned.

A good thought to remember is, "When wise people speak, they make knowledge attractive, but stupid people spout nonsense" (Proverbs 15:2).

Chapter's Challenge:
To learn to choose my words wisely.

"Do not accuse anyone falsely."
— Exodus 20:16

Lies

▼

T o u g h T i m e s :
A lie is a false statement deliberately presented as the truth. A lie is meant to deceive or give the wrong impression. A lie is told to fool people. A lie is saying something you know is not true. Do you agree or disagree with the above statements? _____
Give your reasons. _____

_____

When God gave Moses the Ten Commandments he was setting a standard. He wanted his people to live by this standard. The standard is to speak honestly or always tell the truth about another person.

Once a word is spoken, it cannot be taken back. When you use words to exaggerate or stretch the truth, that is lying. When you only tell half the truth, that is lying. When you lie, you misrepresent the one you are talking about. Lying helps no one, not even the liar. Share the last time you did not tell the truth about something.

_____

What did your lie do? _____

_____

Who was hurt the most by your lie? _____

_____

Was anyone helped by your lie? _____

_____

Why did you lie? _____

_____

Staying Cool:

Watching from her front window, Mrs. Parks saw Jason running home from the bus stop with tears on his face. Mary and a friend were laughing as they stood at the bus stop. "Something must have happened to cause the boy not to wait for the school bus."

What Mrs. Parks missed was the conversation between Jason and Mary. Mary accused Jason of cheating on the history test. Jason called her a liar. Mary laughed at him as she said, "I'm going to get you in trouble."

Jason was shocked at Mary's words. He knew he hadn't cheated. He wondered who his teacher would believe. The more Mary teased, the louder she got. Before long everyone at the bus stop was looking at him.

"You know you're lying. Why don't you just shut up?" Jason was trying to be cool, but he was failing. Finally he picked up his books and ran toward his house.

The other kids immediately started asking about Jason. "Mary, are you sure he cheated?" Mary just smiled as she boarded the school bus.

Good News:

"Keep from speaking evil and from telling lies" (Psalm 34:13).

Quiet Time:

Lord, help me not to say untrue things about others. Help me to always be honest. When others tell lies about me, help me know how to respond.

"Do not use my name for evil purposes, for I the LORD your God will punish anyone who misuses my name."
— Exodus 20:7

Profanity

▼

Tough Times:
Tell what you think the word *profanity* means: _____

_____

If you said that it was the use of abusive, vulgar, or irreverent language, you are right. When you use God's name in a disrespectful or dirty way, you are profaning or dishonoring God.

The third commandment (Exodus 20:7) is a strong warning about the kinds of words you should use with God's name. When a person takes the Lord's name and uses it in the wrong way, then the verse tells you that God will_____.
Misuse of God's name shows a person's true beliefs and character.

In Old Testament times, a name was understood to represent one's personality. God's name is holy. It tells of God's power and greatness. To use God's name in vain or as a curse is a sin. As a Christian you should never give another person reason to lose respect for God because of the way you use His name.

When was the last time you heard God's name used in a way that you knew was wrong? _____

What did you do about what you heard? _____

_____

Do you ever use profanity? Do your words reflect your beliefs and your true character? _____

Staying Cool:

As T. J. slammed the door he let out a string of words that burned his brother's ears. "Wait a minute!" T. J.'s older brother Tony yelled. "Where did you learn to talk like that?"

T. J. just laughed. "It's no big deal."

"Do you know what those words mean?" Tony asked, surprised. He'd never heard T. J. talk like that.

Tony began to question T. J. "Who have you been hanging around? I think someone has been a bad influence."

T. J. and Tony continued to talk about the words that he was using. Tony explained to T. J. that when he chose to use the Lord's name in a bad way he was dishonoring God. T. J. was surprised that Tony was upset. He had never taken an interest in anything he'd said before. "Why do you care how I talk?"

"Well, T. J., I care about you. I don't want you to get in the habit of using those words. It doesn't sound nice, but more important, God doesn't want you to talk like that."

Tony continued while he had his brother's attention. "I know you love God and don't want to dishonor Him. Next time you start to use those words, remember that God is listening and will be displeased."

Good News:

"May my words and my thoughts be acceptable to you" (Psalm 19:4).

Quiet Time:

Dear Lord, help me to keep my thoughts pure so that the words from my mouth might show my love for You.

A gossip can never keep a secret. Stay away from people who talk too much.
— Proverbs 20:19

Gossip

▼

Tough Times:

Gossip is talk that is untrue and unkind. When people talk about something they don't have firsthand knowledge of, be careful how much you believe.

Are rumors gossip? _____ Think of a rumor (something passed on as truth with no proof) that you have heard recently. What affect did the rumor have on what happened?_____

_____

The tongue's power is awesome. It can have a positive affect or a negative affect on people's lives. How you choose to handle rumors and gossip will tell a lot about your character. If you spread rumors or gossip, what does that say about your character? _____

_____

What would cause a person to start a rumor or to spread gossip?

_____

Have you ever been guilty of gossiping? Tell what happened.

_____

The last part of the verse from Proverbs 20:19 says to stay away from people who talk too much. How does the company you keep influence what you say? _____

_____

Staying Cool:

"Ring! Ring!" The phone at Robin's house was ringing as she came in from school. "Hello," Robin answered out of breath.

"Have I got some juicy news for you." Sue was so anxious to tell Robin her news that she didn't want to wait for Robin to put her books down. I heard that Craig and Billy were caught throwing something away in the dumpster behind school."

"So what?" Robin answered, disgusted with Sue. "What's so bad about throwing garbage away in the dumpster?"

Sue just laughed. "Well, I heard it wasn't just any old garbage. They were caught with a package of cigarettes and a lighter."

"You're kidding," Robin responded. "Who caught them and what's going to happen to them?"

"Mr. Clark, the assistant principal, was leaving early and saw them go around the back of the building. He followed them. When he saw them pull something out of their pocket, he yelled for them to stop."

Robin was listening closely to every detail. She was thinking she would call Cheryl to fill her in on this "juicy" piece of news.

Good News:

"A person who obeys God in everything and always does what is right, whose words are true and sincere, . . . he does no wrong to his friends nor spreads rumors about his neighbors" (Psalm 15:2–3).

Quiet Time:

Help me, Lord, never to be guilty of starting rumors or spreading gossip. Help me learn to keep quiet.

Getting involved in an argument that is none of your business is like going down the street and grabbing a dog by the ears.
— Proverbs 26:17

Busybody

▼

Tough Times:

Read the verse above again. Have you ever grabbed a dog by the ear? Think about how the dog would react and why.

A busybody is someone who sticks his or her nose into someone else's business. Another definition of a busybody is one who meddles. Do you know any busybodies? Describe what they do.

_____

Have you ever been accused of being a busybody? Tell about it.

_____

_____

_____

_____

What was lost when you meddled? _____

_____

_____

Staying Cool:

It had been an especially hectic day and Julie was trying hard to finish her project. She really didn't have time for any interruptions. She just wanted to finish and go to bed.

Julie's twin, John, walked by balancing his completed project in the palm of his hand. "Looks like you're not going to finish before the year 2001!"

"Shut up!" Julie yelled. "I don't need your smart mouth."

John just laughed as he continued on down the hall. "Hey, Dad, Julie's goofing off."

Julie wanted to ignore her brother, but it was getting harder all the time. He loved to make her life miserable. He was always sticking his nose in her business and then acting like he was trying to help. "You better mind your own business, John," Julie yelled from her bedroom.

It wasn't long before her dad came by to check on her progress. "Need any help finishing up?"

Julie began to cry as she looked up at her dad. "This is a mess! I can't make it look right and, besides, John is driving me crazy. Make him leave me alone!"

Good News:

"Lord, place a guard at my mouth, a sentry at the door of my lips" (Psalm 141:3).

Quiet Time:

Help me, Lord, know the difference between helping and being a busybody.

A hypocrite hides his hate behind flattering words.
— Proverbs 26:24

Flattery

▼

T o u g h   T i m e s :
Read Proverbs 26:23–28. The six words below on the left will help you understand what flattery is and what it does. Match the words with the correct definitions.

Insincere	damage or destroy
Hypocrite	dislike
Flattery	dishonest
Hate	pretender
Disguise	praise too much
Ruin	hide

These verses help you understand that flattery has no value. Sometimes it is used as sarcasm to make fun of someone. False flattery can give a false impression of your feelings. It hurts the speaker and the person being spoken to.

Verse 23 says that when words are used to spread information that can bring sorrow, they are like a cheap piece of pottery. Even when it is covered with something to make it look better, it is really worthless. Flattering words are worthless too.

Tell about a time when someone used flattery on you to cover up some other feelings. _____

_____

Tell about a time when you used flattery. _____

_____

Staying Cool:

"Oh, Paula, you look so cute. I just love that outfit. You always wear the coolest clothes." Jeanne was always calling attention to Paula's clothes.

"Thanks, I got this last weekend at the mall. I just had to have it!" Paula's clothes were really different and everyone noticed them.

Jeanne didn't have to tell Paula she liked her clothes because it was obvious to everyone that she wouldn't be caught dead in them. Jeanne was always making fun of Paula's clothes when she wasn't around. It was almost like Jeanne was playing a game with Paula. The more Jeanne complimented, the wilder the outfits. Everyone was laughing at Paula and her clothes.

Tell the rest of the story by showing what you think happens to Jeanne when Paula realized what's been happening. _____

_____

_____

Good News:

"All of them lie to one another; they deceive each other with flattery" (Psalm 12:2).

Quiet Time:

Lord, please help me resist the temptation to speak anything but the truth.

Any fool can start arguments; the honorable thing is to stay out of them.
— Proverbs 20:3

Arguing

▼

Tough Times:
Today you will make two acrostics with the word *argument.*

On the first, list people you argue with (possible answers: parents, teachers, mothers, fathers, friends, etc.).

On the second acrostic, list things you argue about. Make sure you find a word for each letter (possible answers: eating, sports, clothing, cleaning up, homework, money, telephone, bedtime, TV).

#1	#2
A	A
R	R
G	G
U	U
M	M
E	E
N	N
T	T

Staying Cool:

You have now identified people you argue with and things you argue about. Write about your last argument. Tell who it was with, why you argued, and what was accomplished by arguing.

_____

_____

_____

_____

_____

_____

Now tell how you could have avoided this argument and how things might have turned out differently.

_____

_____

_____

_____

_____

Do you need to apologize for something you said or did that was hurtful? Maybe you need to talk to God about how you seem to argue about everything that happens and ask Him to help you avoid arguments in the future.

Good News:

"Turn away from evil and do good; strive for peace with all your heart" (Psalm 34:14).

Quiet Time:

Lord, I know that arguments don't really accomplish anything. Help me to be a peacemaker, not one always looking to argue.

A good man's words are wise, and he is always fair.
— Psalm 37:30

A Blessing!

▼

Tough Times:

Go back to the introduction of this chapter. Look over your "Top Ten" list of ways you use words. What do you think about your list? In this chapter you have looked at six ways to use words that can be hurtful or bad. You could probably think of others like tattling, boasting or bragging, putting someone down, or picking on another.

In the space below, tell how you should use words in a positive way instead, and what you will do differently in your life to use words wisely.

_____

_____

_____

_____

The Bible contains many warnings about the words that come out of the mouth. Remember that you should choose your words wisely because you will be held accountable for each one.

Staying Cool:
Design a "Graffiti Wall" that shows what you have learned about
the use of words (a graffiti wall consists of words, phrases, and/or
pictures placed randomly in a space).

Good News:
"A good man's words are wise, and he is always fair"
(Psalm 37:30).

Quiet Time:
Lord, make my words wise and fair in all situations.

Chapter Eight

School Days

▼

Have you ever stopped to figure out how much time you spend in school each year? How many days are required by law? _____ You may need to ask one of your teachers. Do you learn things while in school other than what your teacher teaches? Share your feelings about school.

_____

_____

_____

_____

_____

_____

_____

_____

Growing up you will have some of your best and some of your worst experiences at school. Stop now and list what you consider your three best and your three worst school experiences.

BEST   WORST

_____

_____

_____

_____

_____

_____

_____

_____

In this chapter you will look at how David went from youngest son and shepherd boy to the greatest king of Israel. David faced many challenging times as he grew up. As you look at David's challenging times you will discover ways to handle the challenges that you face during your school days.

Chapter's Challenge:
To learn to face challenges at school.

Then he asked him, "Do you have any more sons?" Jesse answered, "There is still the youngest, but he is out taking care of the sheep." "Tell him to come here," Samuel said.
— 1 Samuel 16:11

Making a Choice

▼

Tough Times:

Samuel, the prophet, was sent by God to Bethlehem to choose (anoint) a man to be the next King of Israel. This was not something Samuel wanted to do, but Samuel went anyway.

When Samuel arrived in Bethlehem, he invited the elders to meet with him (1 Samuel 16:4). He also invited Jesse and his sons. As Samuel looked at each one of Jesse's sons, God let him know that the next king was not among them (1 Samuel 16:10).

Open your Bible to 1 Samuel 16. Read verses 1–10 to better understand what took place. Samuel was sent to pick the next king, but he was having trouble finding the right person. In verse 11 Samuel asked Jesse if he had any more sons. What was Jesse's reply?

_____

David was the youngest. He was the carefree shepherd who was out on a hillside tending his father's sheep. David was not the best-known son. Why do you think God wanted Samuel to pick David to be the next king? _____

_____

Staying Cool:

"Changing schools is the worst," Tommy shouted.

"I don't know any of the teachers. I don't know many of the kids. I don't know how to use a locker. What about eating lunch? Gym class can be scary. What about riding that bus across town?" There was so much bothering Tommy. How could he know he'd made the right choice?

Tommy's mom listened patiently for a few minutes. "Okay, Tommy, I think I know how you feel. Let's stop and talk about the reasons you chose this school."

Tommy flopped down on a chair as his mother handed him a pencil and paper. "Not another list."

Mom smiled. "Everyone has to change schools this year. You decided you wanted to meet some kids whose interests were more like yours. Now it's your turn."

Tommy added that he wanted to take more math and science courses. He could only get the courses at this one school. After writing a few minutes, Tommy was surprised at his lengthy list. "Mom, thanks for stopping me. You've helped me know I've made the right choice. Thanks!"

Choosing a new school can be difficult. The first thing Tommy and his mother did was make a list. Making the list helped Tommy remember the reasons for his choice and understand why his choice was right.

Good News:

"Always be ready to help me, because I follow your commands" (Psalm 119:173).

Quiet Time:

Thank You, God, for giving me the opportunity to make choices. I know, Lord, that You are always there to help me.

The LORD said to Samuel, "This is the one — anoint him!" Samuel took
the olive oil and anointed David in front of his brothers.
— I Samuel 16:12–13

The One!

▼

Tough Times:

Turn to 1 Samuel 16:1. What did God tell Samuel to take to
Bethlehem? _____

Verse 13 tells that "Samuel took the olive oil and anointed David."

Anoint means to smear ointment or pour oil on the head or
body of a person or object. It was usually done for the purpose of
setting a person or object apart for service to the Lord. David
received a special appointment that carried with it no title or office
at that time. Samuel's anointment of David represented what
David would do in the future. Look again at 1 Samuel 16:13 to
find out who took control of David's life.

What difference did it make that God had control of David's
life? What difference does it make when God has control in your
life? Use the space below to tell how you rely on God's help in your
everyday life.

_____

_____

_____

Staying Cool:

Tommy quickly got into the swing of things at Northside Middle School. They expected a lot and you had to do well to stay there, but Tommy already knew that.

The school work was hard. Tommy studied several hours every night, but he didn't mind. He was learning so many new things. For the first time he wasn't bored with school.

Tommy's parents were invited to a parent/teacher conference at the end of the first grading period. Tommy was getting high marks. His hard work was paying off.

Mr. Smith, one of Tommy's teachers, said, "It's really nice having Tommy in class. He is always prepared and has good things to share with the class. He's always very polite. I know you are very proud of him."

That evening as the family ate dinner, Dad told Tommy about the conference. "You know we've always been proud of you, but today it was especially nice to hear how well you've handled the change of schools. We knew you were capable of doing the work."

List the things in this story that let you know Tommy made the right choice. Do you always know the choice you've made is the right one? How? _____

_____

_____

_____

_____

Good News:

"Trust in the Lord. . . . He helps you and protects you" (Psalm 115:9).

Quiet Time:

Thank You, Lord, for the promise that You will always be with me. Help me to rely on Your help everyday.

Then Saul sent a message to Jesse: "I like David. Let him stay here in my service."
— I Samuel 16:22

Popularity Costs?

▼

T o u g h   T i m e s :
David's life was about to change. Read 1 Samuel 16:14–23. One of Saul's men told the king that Jesse's son, David, was a good musician. List the five things said about David in verse 18.

_____ , _____ , _____ ,

_____ , _____ .

    Saul sent a messenger to ask Jesse to_____ .
Jesse obeyed the king's request. In verse 21, what did Saul say that lets you know his feelings about David? _____

_____

    David was becoming a favorite in Saul's court. Saul showed how David pleased him by allowing David to carry his weapons. Look at verse 22 to discover the second message Saul sent Jesse.

_____

    David was favored because he did his best and he pleased the king. Did David do his best to become the favorite? No, David did his best because he knew that was what was expected.

Staying Cool:

The most popular kids all hung out together. Tommy heard talk during lunch about parties on the weekends or going to the mall. The teachers seemed to know the favorites too.

After several weeks a few of them began to talk to Tommy. At first they talked about school stuff and his grades. Then they wanted to know where he lived and if both his parents worked. Before long they asked about his other friends. There were so many questions. The questions made Tommy uncomfortable.

After arriving home one afternoon, Tommy decided he needed help. "Hey, Mom, you got a few minutes? Can we sit down and talk?"

Tommy's mom stopped her work. "What's on your mind?"

"I'm feeling a little uneasy about some things at school. I'm not sure what's really happening."

Tommy continued telling his mom about the questions. "I think I would like to be accepted in the group, but I'm not sure what it will cost me."

Use the space below to tell what you think it could cost Tommy to be accepted by this group of kids.

_____

_____

_____

_____

_____

Good News:

"They will not triumph over me, and I know that you are pleased with me" (Psalm 40:11).

Quiet Time:

Lord, help me know that being popular isn't the most important thing. Help me be like David and do my best.

Jonathan swore eternal friendship with David because of his deep affection for him.
— 1 Samuel 18:3

Friendships

▼

Tough Times:
Open your Bible to 1 Samuel 18. Read verses 1–4. Look over the list of words one the left that describe the friendship between David and Jonathan. Match the words with their definition.

Deeply attracted   commitment
Love   determined attachment
Eternal friendship   heartfelt devotion
Deep affection   never-ending relationship

Jonathan and David had a very special friendship. Verse 5 tells what gifts Jonathan gave to David. Name them. _____

_____

Think about a close friendship that you have with someone. Do any of the words above describe your friendship? Describe your friendship and include what makes your friendship work.

_____

_____

Staying Cool:

It was amazing what was happening. Tommy was in a new school and he was getting lots of attention.

Steve sat next to Tommy in math class. Tommy and Steve had talked a little. One day the teacher called on Steve to solve a problem. Some of the other kids began to laugh and snicker when he had trouble.

When class was over Tommy hung back waiting for Steve to get his stuff together. "Hey, Steve, what are you doing after school? Would you like to come over?"

Astonished, Steve looked up. "You talking to me?"

"Why wouldn't I talk to you?" Tommy couldn't figure this guy out. "Steve, I've been wanting to get to know you, but you haven't acted like you were interested in being friends."

Steve began to mumble something about Tommy not being accepted if he was seen hanging around him. "I know the others want you to be a part of their group. So that means you can't be friends with me."

Do you think Steve is right? Should Tommy not be his friend because of what others think? What do you think? _____

_____

_____

_____

Good News:

"I prayed with my head bowed low, as I would pray for a friend" (Psalm 36:13–14).

Quiet Time:

Thank You, Lord, for my friends. Help me to do what I need to keep my friendships strong. Help me to remember to pray for my friends.

And so he was jealous and suspicious of David from that day on.
— I Samuel 18:9

A Change?

▼

T o u g h T i m e s :
David's success against Goliath made him very popular with the people of Israel. They sang joyful songs and danced and played instruments to celebrate. King Saul heard their songs and he became angry. What does 1 Samuel 18:8 say the people were saying about King Saul and David? _____

_____

_____

David was facing changes. King Saul was not only jealous of David's popularity, but the king said he would be suspicious of David from that day on. David went from being the favorite to being someone who had to run away and hide.

Read 1 Samuel 18:6–9. You know the king's feelings, but how do you think David might have felt?

Use another sheet of paper to draw a modern-day picture or write about what happens when jealous or envious feelings control someone.

Remember, *jealous* means resenting someone who is more successful than you, someone who has something you want and cannot have.

Staying Cool:

Tommy and Steve were becoming good friends. They spent time together after school. They talked on the phone.

One day at school Tommy noticed Steve was acting funny. "Steve, wait up," Tommy yelled down the hall.

Tommy tried to catch Steve before he went into his next class. It was almost like Steve was ignoring him. Steve avoided Tommy the rest of the day. He managed to miss Tommy's phone call.

Tommy was confused. "What could be the matter?" The next day Tommy waited outside for Steve to arrive. "Morning!"

Tommy was surprised by Steve's behavior. "You're really some friend. I can't believe you're going to the math contest. When were you going to tell me?"

"Is that what's bugging you?" Tommy was in shock. "It's really no big deal."

"Maybe not to you!" Steve stomped off.

Use the space below to tell how jealousy changed this friendship.

_____

_____

_____

_____

_____

_____

_____

Good News:

"Trust in God at all times, my people. Tell him all your troubles" (Psalm 62:8).

Quiet Time:

Lord, help me to try to understand my friends when they get upset about something good that happens to me.

"Is there anyone left of Saul's family to whom I can show loyalty and kindness, as I promised God I would?"
— 2 Samuel 9:3

Lasting Friendship
▼

Tough Times:
Usually when a new king took over, he got rid of all the descendants of the former king. David did not do that when he became king of Israel. In 1 Samuel 20:14–15 you find David and Jonathan's promise to take care of the other's family if one of them should die.

Read 2 Samuel 9:1–13 in your Bible. David was looking for Saul's descendants. What two reasons do the Bible verses give for David's search? (verse 1) _____
(verse 3) _____

Jonathan's son was special. Second Samuel 4:4 tells what made him special. _____

What did David tell Mephibosheth he would do for him (2 Samuel 9:7)? _____

Loyalty (faithfulness) and kindness are very evident in David's treatment of Jonathan's son. What part do loyalty and kindness play in your life? To what or whom are you loyal? _____

_____

_____

What causes you to show kindness to others? _____

_____

Staying Cool:

Today is a new day, thought Tommy. *I'm going to show Steve that I am a true friend even though he chose to be jealous.*

Tommy waited outside the cafeteria for Steve to come to lunch. He stood across the hall out of sight so Steve wouldn't see him. It had been several days since the boys' conversation. Tommy hoped Steve had cooled off.

Finish the story by showing how Tommy's loyalty and kindness toward Steve made a difference, and how Steve responded to Tommy. _____

_____

_____

_____

_____

_____

_____

_____

_____

_____

Good News:

"Your love and loyalty will always keep me safe" (Psalm 40:11).

Quiet Time:

Thank You, Lord, for loyal friends. Help me to show love to my friends by being loyal and kind.

So all the leaders of Israel came to King David at Hebron. He made a sacred alliance with them, they anointed him, and he became king of Israel. David was thirty years old when he became king, and he ruled for forty years.
— 2 Samuel 5:3–4

A Shining Example

▼

Tough Times:

Look closely at the verses above. They say that the leaders of Israel came to ask "King David" to be king of Israel. Are you a little confused? Open your Bible to 2 Samuel 2:4 to find out the name of the land where David first was king. _____

_____

David's popularity had not faded. After many years of conflict with Saul and of being a great warrior, the people still loved and respected David. They wanted him to be king of all Israel.

David was Israel's greatest king. His outstanding characteristic was his devotion (faithfulness) to the Lord. David always gave God all the praise and glory.

Yes, David did have his faults, but God was able to use him regardless of his mistakes. This king was a shining example of what God can do with a life that is committed to Him.

Staying Cool:

Take a few minutes to think about David's life. Then think about your life so far. Is your life committed to God? God can use you in spite of your faults. How are you willing to let God use you? Like David, you too can be a shining example for others. Use the space below to write a prayer of commitment to God.

_____

_____

_____

_____

_____

_____

_____

_____

_____

_____

_____

_____

_____

Good News:

"Give yourself to the Lord; trust in him, and he will help you; he will make your righteousness shine like the noonday sun" (Psalm 37:5–6).

Quiet Time:

Read over your prayer of commitment and thank God for His constant love.

Chapter Nine

Modern-Day Dilemmas

▼

How do you respond when faced with these *tough* circumstances?

The choice is yours! You can ignore the problem in hopes it will go away. You can work for solutions to these tough issues. What or who will guide your decisions?

Use the space to list all the things that could influence what you think and do about these tough situations (example: parents, friends).

_____

_____

_____

_____

_____

_____

_____

_____

_____

_____

Chapter's Challenge:
To make a vow or promise to honestly try to be a part of a solution to as many of these problems as possible.

"I was hungry and you fed me, thirsty and you gave me drink; I was a stranger and you received me in your homes."
— Matthew 25:35

Homeless and Hungry

▼

Tough Times:

Did you know there are stories in the Bible about people being homeless and hungry? The Book of Exodus tells us Moses and the children of Israel wandered in the wilderness for many years. John the Baptist lived in the desert before he began preaching.

Both of these interesting stories tell about what it was like not to have a permanent home. In each of these stories there was a reason for the people to be homeless. Read the story found in Exodus 16:1–30 to find out how God provided the necessary food. Now read the story of John the Baptist in Matthew 3:1–10 to find out where John lived and what he ate.

Many things lead to people being homeless and hungry. What can they do? Where do they turn for help? Will God drop "manna" from heaven like he did for Moses and the children of Israel? Does God expect other people to help provide food and shelter?

Homeless and hungry people represent a very big problem today. Perhaps you have seen someone on a street corner with a sign saying: "will work for food." Should you stop? Should you offer help?

What are some of the things you can do? _____

_____

_____

Staying Cool:

Find a newspaper or magazine article that deals with the homeless and hungry. Read it. Go back and highlight information in the article that will help you make a decision about how you should respond to this tough issue.

A vow is a solemn or serious pledge or promise that you will do something. In the space below write a vow about what you can do to help homeless and hungry people. You may want to share your vow with your family. Maybe as a family you can do something together to make a difference for homeless and hungry people in your community.

_____

_____

_____

_____

_____

_____

_____

Good News:

"May those who are wise think about these things" (Psalm 107:43).

Quiet Time:

Lord, I have to admit that homeless people frighten me. Help me know how I can be more like You in offering help to those who have no home or food.

"Happy are those who work for peace; God will call them his children!"
— Matthew 5:9

War

▼

T o u g h   T i m e s :

When you watch the news on television and see bombs going off and people lying dead in the street, what do you think? Are you glad that isn't happening in your city, town, or country? Tell how you feel about what you see. _____

_____

War is an armed fight between countries or different groups of people within the same country.

Throughout the Old Testament you read about wars. Some of these wars were fought to destroy God's enemies. Other wars were fought to revenge some injury, insult, or offense. Some wars were God's way of allowing His people to possess land. Read about David's fight with the Ammonites in 2 Samuel 10:1–14. Why was there fighting?_____

_____

Why do we have wars today? Is there ever a winner when armed fighting breaks out between two groups of people? Do you know how you feel about war? Share your feelings in the space below. _____

_____

_____

Staying Cool:

Find someone that has fought in a war and interview that person by asking the following questions:

1. In what war did you fight?
2. In what country did the fighting take place?
3. What job did you perform? or
   What did you do during the war?
4. What caused this war?
5. What did this war accomplish? Did anyone win?
6. What was lost because of the war?
7. How were you treated when you returned home?
8. How were things different for you after the war?
9. What did you learn from war?

What did you learn from this interview about war? Share your feelings. Do you sometimes feel like you're "going to war" with a friend or family member? How can you make peace instead?

_____

_____

Good News:

"Strive for peace with all your heart" (Psalm 34:14).

Quiet Time:

Help me, Lord, to be a peacemaker. Help me to be willing to work toward settling differences through peaceful means. No one wins in a war.

Parents, do not treat your children in such a way as to make them angry. Instead, raise them with Christian discipline and instruction.
— Ephesians 6:4

Child Abuse

▼

Tough Times:

Child abuse is bad or wrong treatment of a child. Child abuse comes in many forms, including rude speech or insulting language, physical punishment like hitting or beating, sexual abuse, and neglect like when a child is left alone for long periods of time without proper food, clothing, or shelter. Children today endure many kinds of abuse.

Read Ephesians 6:1–4 to learn about the relationship God expects between parents and their children. What is a child's Christian duty? _____

_____

What is the first commandment that has a promise? _____

_____

What is the promise? _____

_____

Verse 4 is talking to parents. How should children be raised?

_____

Colossians 3:20–21 also tells about the relationship between parents and children. Read those verses now.

These verses are also a warning to adults. Children should obey and respect adults, while adults should treat children with respect and dignity. When this gets out of balance, trouble results.

Staying Cool:

Do children experience abuse from people other than their parents?_____ Do you know anyone that has been abused? _____
Have you experienced abuse from someone? _____

Find an article in a newspaper that tells about an abused child. Read the article. Highlight words in the article that show how the child or children were abused. Mark the name or names of the abuser(s). Think about how the article makes you feel.

How could the abuse in the article have been stopped or prevented?

_____

What can you do about the abuse that you or other children suffer?

_____

If you are experiencing abuse, the most important thing for you to know is that you are not alone. If you don't feel that you can talk to one of your parents, then talk to a teacher at school or church or to your pastor. Help is available. Caring, understanding people want to help you.

Good News:

"Children are a gift from the Lord; they are a real blessing"
(Psalm 127:3).

Quiet Time:

Lord, the next time I'm uncomfortable about what is happening to me or to someone else, help me share those feelings with someone that can help.

Don't you know that your body is the temple of the Holy Spirit, who lives in you and who was given to you by God? You do not belong to yourselves but to God; he bought you for a price. So use your bodies for God's glory.
— 1 Corinthians 6:19–20

Addictions

▼

Tough Times:

What does 1 Corinthians 6:19–20 say to you about your body?

_____

The key verses above say that your body is the "temple of the Holy Spirit." Tell what you think that means. _____

_____

These verses say that you need to be careful about what you put into your body. Verse 20 says God bought you for a price. That means Christ paid the price for your sins when He died for you. Because He did that then, what should you do now with your body?

_____

What does the word *addiction* mean? _____

_____

Addiction comes from the word *addict*. An addict is a person who allows himself or herself to be taken over or controlled by a drug or habit. When people have little or no control over themselves, who or what is responsible for their behavior? Drugs, alcohol, cigarettes, and overeating can all be harmful and addictive.

Staying Cool:

Too often advertisements convince people that certain kinds of behaviors are "cool" and acceptable. They do not show you what happens when a person drinks too much. Do they tell how a junkie feels when the drug is wearing off? They do not say the addict never gets enough. They do not show what a person's lungs look like after smoking cigarettes for years. They do not talk about what happens when you constantly overeat.

Your assignment: Make a collage with pictures from magazine advertisements that promote addictive behavior. Tape, paste, or glue your pictures on another sheet of paper. After you place the pictures, write words that show you understand that these kinds of choices are not ways to glorify God with your body.

Now that you have finished your collage, write a *vow* telling how you will handle possible addictions.

My vow: _____

_____

_____

_____

_____

Good News:

"I have avoided all evil conduct, because I obey your commands" (Psalm 119:101)

Quiet Time:

Lord, sometimes things I see and hear confuse me about how I should use my body. Lord, I want You to be in control of my life, not something else.

Do not conform yourselves to the standards of this world, but let God transform you inwardly by a complete change of your mind. Then you will be able to know the will of God, what is good and is pleasing to him and is perfect.
— Romans 12:2

Television's Influence

▼

Tough Times:
Of all human inventions, probably none has failed more than television to live up to its potential for good. Television is a forceful influence in people's lives. Too many people let television control their time.

The world comes to your living room nightly in the form of news. You live in a day where you see history happening. You don't have to wait and read about it in a textbook years later. Thanks to television, information is passed on quickly, but not always responsibly.

Television has a striking impact on your attitudes, behavior, values, and decisions. Television can shape the way you think and act. The words found in Romans 12:2 tell you to not _____ yourself to the _____ of the world. How does television encourage you to conform to the world?

_____

Staying Cool:
Examine your television habits. On the chart on the next page list your favorite shows, how long they last, and what they are about. Also tell how the show affects you attitude, behavior, or thinking.

Below the chart there is a place to add up how much time you spend watching television each week.

Name of Show	Length of Show	Content	Effects
_____	_____	_____	_____
_____	_____	_____	_____
_____	_____	_____	_____
_____	_____	_____	_____
_____	_____	_____	_____

Total amount of time spent watching television: _____

Who decides what is suitable to watch?_____

Does your family ever talk about programs you watch?_____

What could be accomplished by this kind of discussion?_____

_____

Would these talks help you better understand how to live? Would they help you know what is right, good and pleasing to God?

Write a promise about how much television you will watch and how you will let it affect your character. _____

_____

_____

Good News:

"The Lord rewards me because I do what is right" (Psalm 18:20).

Quiet Time:

Television controls too much of my time, Lord. I don't want it to control my life. Help me to spend my time more wisely with You, my family, and friends.

A person who has a dreaded skin disease must wear torn clothes, leave his hair uncombed, cover the lower part of his face and call out, "Unclean, unclean!" . . . and he must live outside the camp, away from others."
— Leviticus 13:45–46

Today's Lepers
▼

Tough Times:

Leprosy was a term used to describe serious skin diseases. People with leprosy might have white patches on their skin. They might have running or open sores. People with leprosy could lose fingers and toes.

Turn in your Bible to Leviticus 13:1–46 where you will find out how people with leprosy were treated.

People having this dreaded disease were considered unclean (not pure) and were feared. Following is a list of rules for people with this disease:

1. take person to the priest (verse 2)
2. isolate person (verse 4)
3. shave around infected area (verse 33)
4. wear torn clothes (verse 45)
5. leave hair uncombed (verse 45)
6. cover lower part of face (verse 45)
7. call out, "Unclean, unclean!" (verse 45)
8. live away from others (verse 46)

People with leprosy definitely were treated different. Throughout Jesus' ministry he healed people, even those with leprosy. In Luke 17:11–19, read how He healed a group of lepers. How did the lepers respond?

Staying Cool:
Today, what disease do people fear and dread? _____

If you wrote down AIDS, then you are right. How are people with AIDS treated in some of the same ways as the lepers in Bible times?

AIDS (Acquired Immune Deficiency Syndrome): a disease that attacks the body's immune system. (A healthy immune system enables the body to fight other diseases.) AIDS keeps the body from fighting cancer, pneumonia, and many other diseases. It is spread through intimate contacts involving blood or some other body fluids.

Use the space below to express your feelings about AIDS.

_____

_____

Remember that Jesus healed the sick. Jesus cared about people no matter what their sickness or disease. He cared enough to be concerned. Many times he was criticized for getting involved in their lives.

How can you show concern for seriously ill persons? Do you know someone personally who has AIDS? Can you overcome your fears and help someone with AIDS? Can you make a vow concerning your treatment of people with serious diseases?

My vow:_____

Good News:
"You are my God; teach me to do your will. Be good to me and guide me on a safe path" (Psalm 143:10).

Quiet Time:
It's all too easy to judge people with AIDS. Help me, Lord, to find ways to show that I care, and that You care about them.

"I now realize that it is true that God treats everyone on the same basis."
— Acts 10:34

For God judges everyone by the same standard.
— Romans 2:11

Discrimination/Prejudice

▼

Tough Times:

Discrimination is an unfair difference in treatment. People discriminate against others when they treat them differently without a proper reason. A similar word is prejudice. *Prejudice* is an opinion that is formed about someone or something without good reason.

Both of these words are a part of your life today. Look closely at the two Scripture passages above. What are they telling you? _____

_____

Why do discrimination and prejudice exist today? _____

_____

Name some of today's victims of discrimination and prejudice. ____

_____

How can prejudice and discrimination be stopped? Turn to James 2:8 to find the answer. _____

_____

Staying Cool:

Think about what you have learned in this chapter. Tell how prejudice and discrimination affect your response to the following situations:

1. Homeless or hungry people in your community —

2. Overweight people —

3. Foreigners in your school —

4. People of other races —

5. People who commit crimes —

6. Strangers —

7. People with AIDS —

Remember, "God treats everyone on the same basis." How can you begin treating people like God does? Write your own vow showing how you want to relate to people who are different from you. _____

_____

_____

Good News:

"The Lord loves those who hate evil; he protects the lives of his people; he rescues them from the power of the wicked" (Psalm 97:10).

Quiet Time:

Lord, forgive me when I treat others differently or unfairly because of some prejudice.

Chapter Ten

Setbacks

▼

Many things happen to you that might be considered a setback. The term *setback* may be new to you. Look closely at the definition.

A *setback* is an unwelcome change in your life or it is something that interrupts your life.

Make a list of the things you think might be setbacks:

_____

_____

_____

_____

_____

_____

_____

In this chapter you will look at six setbacks in Joseph's life that God used to work out His plan. Many times Joseph was the victim.

A *victim* is a person that is injured, ruined, killed, cheated, or tricked. The way Joseph responded made the difference. Joseph remained true to God by the way he handled his setbacks. This allowed God to use the bad things that happened and turn them into something good.

Joseph's story is found in Genesis. Keep your Bible close as you go through this chapter.

Chapter's Challenge:
To remain true to God.

"Do you think you are going to be king and rule over us?" his brothers asked. So they hated him even more because of his dreams and because of what he said about them.
— Genesis 37:8

Sibling Rivalry

▼

Tough Times:
Joseph had eleven brothers. Their resentment and strong feelings of dislike made for a troubled family. Find Genesis 37:2–11. Read the verses to discover the reasons for the rivalry. List three reasons you found.

_____

_____

Your first impression of Joseph might be that he caused the problems. The trouble really started when his father treated him as the favorite son. Reread verse 3. What words tell of this problem? _____

In verse 5 Joseph had a _____ and he told his brothers

he would be a _____ and _____.
Joseph's ability to interpret dreams did not improve his relationship with his brothers.

Joseph had a second dream (verse 9). The brothers did not like this dream either. Joseph told them that even the _____,

_____, and _____ would bow down to him.

Who else was upset when Joseph told him about this dream?

_____

Sibling rivalry existed in this family. The brothers' response of hatred and Joseph's attitude contributed to this setback. How was Joseph the victim in this story? _____

_____

Staying Cool:

Read the following story and write an ending that shows how your attitude toward other family members could be a setback for you.

Jason's older brother and sister, Jake and Julie, were tops in everything. Everybody was always praising them for something wonderful they did. This was especially hard for Jason. He felt like he couldn't measure up.

After a really tough day at school, Jason ran to his room and slammed the door. He lay on the bed thinking. The longer he lay there, the madder he got. He jumped up and ran out of his room yelling for his sister. "I can't believe you would do that to me. I was so embarrassed. Why? Why? Why?"

Julie was in the kitchen telling her mom about what happened when the yelling started. "Mom . . . _____

_____

_____

Good News:

"Create a pure heart in me, O God, and put a new and loyal spirit in me" (Psalm 51:10).

Quiet Time:

Lord, many times I want to blame others for the bad things that happen, when all along my attitude was the problem. Forgive me for the troubles I cause in my family.

"Just throw him into this well in the wilderness, but don't hurt him."...

When some Midianite traders came by, the brothers pulled Joseph out of the well and sold him for twenty pieces of silver.
— Genesis 37:22,28

Taken Away

▼

Tough Times:

Genesis 37:12–28 tells the story of how Joseph lost his family. Read about the sad chain of events in these verses. One thing led to another and before Rueben, the oldest brother, could stop the others, Joseph was gone.

In this story Joseph obeyed his father. He was sent out to see if his brothers were safe and if the flocks were all right. After many days of searching for his brothers he finally located them. The brothers saw him coming. They were still angry over the dreams. Who kept them from killing Joseph? _____ How?

_____

In a few short hours Joseph went from favorite son to slave.

Joseph must have had all kinds of mixed feelings: shock, fear, disappointment, and sadness were probably only some. This turn of events was definitely a setback. Joseph once again was a victim. Tell how you think he is a victim in this story. _____

_____

_____

Staying Cool:

It must be the middle of the night, Jenny thought when the phone woke her. She listened to see if everything was all right. *Who could be calling?*

After a few minutes, Jenny was dreaming again. She saw flashing lights bouncing off a wet street. She heard strange voices. As Jenny tossed and turned, her dream continued. Her dad was telling a policeman she was missing. Jenny tried to yell out, but her dad didn't hear her. Shaking in her bed, Jenny tried to wake up, but the nightmare continued.

Jenny didn't understand why they thought she'd gone. *What has happened to me?* Jenny wondered from her dream, *I can't be gone.*

The next morning when Jenny woke up, she sat up and rubbed her eyes as she looked at the clock. She remembered her dream. Jenny ran downstairs to find her mom.

Tell how you would feel if you had been Jenny. How would you feel if you were taken away from your family?

_____

_____

_____

_____

_____

_____

Good News:

"I call to you in times of trouble, because you answer my prayers" (Psalm 86:7).

Quiet Time:

Lord, I know that You are always with me even when I find myself in situations that I don't understand.

*[Reuben] returned to his brothers and said, "The boy is not there!
What am I going to do?". . . [Jacob said,] "Some wild animal has
killed him. My son Joseph has been torn to pieces!"*
— Genesis 37:30,33

No Hope

▼

Tough Times:

Open your Bible to Genesis 37. Read verses 29–36 to discover who
lost hope and why.

Did you find that at first Reuben lost hope? Reuben lost hope
when he came back to the well and found Joseph gone. The brothers made matters worse when they decided to lie to their father
about what happened to Joseph.

Their father showed his hopelessness when he tore his clothes in
sorrow and put on sackcloth. Jacob was mourning the death of his son.

This was definitely a setback in Joseph's life. His family would be
lost to him forever. This time Joseph was a victim of his brothers' lies.

Have you ever lost hope? Have you ever felt like you were the
victim of someone else's lies? Share your experience and your feelings.

_____

_____

_____

_____

Staying Cool:

"GUN-CARRYING STUDENT
BRINGS CLASS TO A STANDSTILL!"

As Mrs. Davis read the headline, she looked up and asked, "What's happening to our kids that they would think of using a gun like this? Where were the parents?"

Mrs. Davis sat quietly reading the article. Shaking her head in disbelief, she said, "This boy was upset over his report card. Why would someone so young immediately turn to this kind of violence to settle a problem with grades?"

She continued telling her husband about the article. "This young man took his father's loaded gun out of his drawer and put it in his backpack. He waited till class had started and then jumped up and began yelling at the teacher. He pulled the gun from the backpack and started shooting at the ceiling. Can you just imagine the panic in that room?"

Use the rest of this space to tell why you think young people would turn to guns to resolve their problems. Do you think they might feel hopeless? What effect would that have on your story?

_____

_____

_____

_____

_____

Good News:
"We put our hope in the Lord; he is our protector and our help" (Psalm 33:20).

Quiet Time:
Lord, because of my belief in You, I know that I can live a life full of hope. Help me to share that hope.

Now the Ishmaelites had taken Joseph to Egypt and sold him to Potiphar, one of the king's officers who was the captain of the palace guard.
— Genesis 39:1

Hard Time

▼

Tough Times:

Joseph was now owned by another man. He was no longer that favorite son. He was a slave. His owner was the captain of the palace guard.

Joseph experienced quite a change from the life he had at home. Again, Joseph faced a setback in his life.

Read Genesis 39:1–6 to learn about Joseph's new life. Verse 3 tells that the _____ was with Joseph and made him _____ in everything he did. Potiphar was pleased with his new slave and made him his _____. Joseph was now put in charge of Potiphar's house and everything he owned.

Again Joseph's circumstances changed. He didn't let this setback make him a victim. Joseph responded in a positive way by successfully doing the work he was given. He showed Potiphar that he could handle responsibility.

When you are faced with hard times, how do your respond? Do they make you a victim or do you try to make the best of the situation? _____

Staying Cool:

Donna's family planned to spend a weekend in the mountains. There was no school the following Monday so the family would get in an extra day of skiing. Everyone was really excited.

The weekend before the trip, Donna's dad called a family meeting. Dad didn't look very happy. "I'm afraid we will have to cancel our plans for the skiing trip." After a few moans of disappointment, they listened to the reasons for the change in plans.

Dad continued, "I have something I need to tell you. There have been some changes at my work, and they no longer need me. I have to find a new job. I think it is best if we don't spend the money on skiing this weekend. We may need it for something more important later."

Before Donna could say anything, her mom began telling them that things would have to be different until their father found another job.

Donna was about to experience changes in her lifestyle. Finish the story by telling how Donna could respond positively to the change in her family. Think about how you would respond in a similar situation. _____

_____

_____

_____

_____

Good News:

"God is our shelter and strength, always ready to help in times of trouble" (Psalm 46:1).

Quiet Time:

Lord, help me to accept the changes that will come in my life, even when I don't like or understand them.

"That Hebrew slave that you brought here came into my room and insulted me. But when I screamed, he ran outside, leaving his robe beside me."
— Genesis 39:17–18

Falsely Accused
▼

Tough Times:

This setback in Joseph's life seems so unfair that you almost get angry. People too often are accused unfairly just because someone wants to get back at them. Sometimes you don't know who to believe.

Read this story in Genesis 39:6–18. Describe the scene at Potiphar's house._____

_____

Why did Joseph refuse Potiphar's wife? (verses 8–9)

_____

What did the wife do that got Joseph in trouble?

_____

Why did the wife falsely accuse Joseph?

_____

Joseph was once again facing a setback. He was a victim when this woman unfairly tried to get back at him. Has someone tried to unfairly get back at you? What happened? Share your experience.

_____

_____

_____

Staying Cool:

Even though her mom wasn't home, Lisa had two friends coming over after school. Lisa's mom trusted them.

As the group got off the bus, Megan announced she'd see them later. "Where are you going?" Lisa yelled as Megan ran after Terri.

Lisa and Patty were talking about Megan's disappearing act when her mom arrived home early. "Hey, girls, how's everything going?"

Mom saw Lisa's surprised expression. "How come you're home so early?" Lisa was worried about what would happen next.

"I thought Megan was supposed to be with you two girls," Mom said as she took off her coat. "What happened to her?"

Lisa looked at Patty, then at her mom, "Oh, she decided to go to Terri's instead."

"Now, Lisa, you know that I trusted all of you to come straight here after school. If I hadn't come home early I would never have known. I guess I can't trust you after all. You're grounded for a week."

Finish the story by telling what Lisa can do to make her mom understand what happened. _____

_____

_____

_____

Good News:

"Declare me innocent, O Lord, because I do what is right and trust you completely" (Psalm 26:1).

Quiet Time:

Lord, help me remain true to You even when I find myself being accused of something I didn't do. Help me to make others understand.

Joseph's master was furious and had Joseph arrested and put in the prison where the king's prisoners were kept, and there he stayed.
— Genesis 39:19–20

Punished though Innocent

▼

T o u g h   T i m e s :
What else could happen to Joseph? He went from favorite son, to slave, to personal servant, to prisoner. Every time Joseph seemed to be making the best out of a bad situation, something happened that was a setback.

Joseph might have even been depressed and angry about this change; after all, he had done nothing wrong. How did Joseph respond? Read Genesis 39:21–23. Verse 21 tells you again that the Lord was with Joseph and blessed him. While in prison, Joseph made a new friend who helped him. What does verse 22 tell you that Joseph was put in charge of? _____

It wasn't fair that Joseph was punished for something he didn't do. Verses 21–23 let you know that even in this unfair situation God was working things out for Joseph.

Tell about a time when you were punished for something you didn't do. How did you respond? _____

_____

_____

Staying Cool:

Eddie felt all alone in his new surroundings. He spent every afternoon in the new apartment by himself while his mother worked. His dad was away all week working a new job.

No one at the new school wanted to be his friend. Life was terrible. Why did everything have to change? *I liked things the way they were,* Eddie thought about what he was missing as he sat in the lonely apartment.

The ringing of the telephone interrupted Eddie's thoughts. "I'm sure it's a wrong number," he said to himself. "I'll let the machine get it."

An unfamiliar voice on the line said, "Hey, Eddie, this is Ken! We're in several classes together. Remember, I said I'd call."

Eddie jumped up, grabbed the phone, and yelled, "Hang on a minute! Let me turn off the machine."

Ken told Eddie about a skating party his Sunday School class was having the next week. "I would really like you to come. After the party we're going to have a lockin at Mr. Pat's house. You'll really like him; he's great."

Eddie had felt like he was being punished unfairly when his parents had to move away. Things began to change when Ken showed he wanted to be Eddie's friend. Share your feeling about this story. Did Eddie have a right to feel the way he did?

Good News:

"You are near to me, O LORD" (Psalm 119:151).

Quiet Time:

God, I know that You are always with me. Help me to understand the unfair things that happen and to not feel like I am always being punished.

"You plotted evil against me, but God turned it into good, in order to preserve the lives of many people who are alive today because of what happened."
— Genesis 50:20

Good out of Evil

▼

Tough Times:

Joseph did experience some setbacks in his life. The setbacks were almost unbearable. Throughout Joseph's life, God continued to turn the bad things (setbacks) into good. Joseph's setbacks became stepping stones for God to work out his plan. Read over the list of Joseph's setbacks.

1. Sibling rivalry
2. Taken away from family
3. Slavery
4. Falsely accused
5. Punished when innocent
6. Loss of hope

Now go back and read over your list of set backs in the introduction to this chapter. Use the lines below to share about one setback in your life. What were the results of the experience? What could you have done differently that would have allowed God to turn the setback into something good?

_____

_____

_____

_____

_____

_____

Staying Cool:

Many times things happen that change or interrupt your life. God can change those bad things (setbacks) to good in your life.

Write a prayer asking God to help you find and do the good things you should even when faced with setbacks. Make sure you share with God your feelings of both joy and disappointment.

_____

_____

_____

_____

_____

_____

_____

Good News:

"Go to the Lord for help; and worship him continually"
Psalm 105:4).

Quiet Time:

Thank You, God, for showing me that You will always be with me and for always keeping Your promises.

Chapter Eleven

An Advertisement!

▼

This chapter will help you explore the idea of you being an advertisement for your family, yourself, your school, your friends, your church, and for God. You will look at the life of the New Testament prophet John the Baptist. John was Jesus' advertisement.

An *advertisement* is an announcement that describes what is special or good about something or someone. Advertisements are made to get people to buy a product, use a service, or to support a person or cause.

What kind of advertisement are you? On the next page, paste a picture of you and your family. Below the picture write a brief description of each person by labeling (naming) each person and telling their relationship to you. Also tell what makes your family special.

_____

_____

_____

Chapter's Challenge:
To be a good advertisement for God.

There was a priest named Zechariah, who belonged to the priestly order of Abijah. His wife's name was Elizabeth; she also belonged to a priestly family. They both lived good lives in God's sight and obeyed fully all the Lord's laws and commands."
— Luke 1:5–6

Family Tree

▼

Tough Times:

Open your Bible to Luke. Today you will search Luke 1 for words that tell about this family:

Mother's name: _____ (Luke 1:5)

Father's name: _____ (Luke 1:5)

Father's occupation: _____ (Luke 1:8)

Aunt's name: _____ (Luke 1:36)

Cousin's name: _____ (Luke 1:31)

Elizabeth named her baby: _____ (Luke 1:60)

Who rejoiced with family: _____ (Luke 1:58)

Read the whole story in Luke 1:5–66 to better understand what was happening with this family.

Write an advertisement about John the Baptist's family in the space below. Use words you found in the Scripture passage that help you describe this family. Remember, an advertisement is an announcement describing what is special or good about something or someone. _____

_____

_____

Staying Cool:

"Rise and shine! Breakfast is on the table," Mrs. Lawrence called upstairs. "It's Sunday!"

As the whole family gathered around a steaming plate of bacon and pancakes, everyone started grabbing before they even sat down. Sunday mornings were hectic. "Wait just one minute. Haven't we forgotten something?" Dad asked them to bow their heads. "Thank You, Lord, for this new day. Help us remember Your goodness to us. Thank You for this food. May it nourish our bodies. Amen."

As the family ate, they talked about the day. "Please remember this morning to take your Bible and Sunday School books along with your offering. We will leave in exactly thirty minutes. I don't want us to be late," Mom said as the children were leaving the table.

The Lawrences were faithful church members. They worshiped together each week and enjoyed their Bible study classes. Several of the children's friends found it hard to believe they went to church every week. They were even more surprised that they liked church.

How does your family advertise church? Do you attend regularly? Do you enjoy going? How do you talk about your church? What does your family's church attendance say about your beliefs?

_____

_____

_____

_____

_____

Good News:

"Praise the Lord our God; worship before his throne! Holy is he!" (Psalm 99:5).

Quiet Time:

Help me to remember that when I faithfully go to church, I am telling others of my belief in You.

"You, my child, will be called a prophet of the Most High God. You will go ahead of the Lord to prepare his road for him."
— Luke 1:76

Promise and Potential

▼

T o u g h   T i m e s :
John was promised to Zechariah and Elizabeth when they were very old. Read Luke 1:15–17 to find out what the angel Gabriel said to Zechariah about this child. What made John a child of promise?

_____

Zechariah was excited about the birth of this child. John's name means "the Lord is gracious." John's parents knew God had been good to them.

Read the father's words of praise in Luke 1:67–79. The first eight verses tell what God had done and what He promised He would do. Verses 76–79 are about the mission his son John would undertake. Zechariah had a good understanding of what his son would do.

Luke 1:80 tells that John grew and developed in both _____ and _____. Where did John live until he started preaching? _____

When children are born, it is appropriate to praise God. Parents today have expectations for their children, just like John's father. All children have potential. If you don't know your parents' hopes and dreams for your life, talk with them now.

Staying Cool:

You are a child of promise and potential. Today you will have the opportunity to share your feelings about who you are and what you can become. First, what are your parents hope and dreams for your life? _____

_____

Second, what are your hopes and dreams for your life?

_____

_____

Do you believe you have potential? _____ If you do, then you can become all that is expected with hard work and determination. What are you doing now to reach your full potential? _____

_____

_____

First, are you meeting your parents' expectations?_____

Second, are you meeting your expectations?_____

Third, can you meet both expectations?_____
Write an advertisement about you. Tell what is special and good about you. Tell about your potential. Be honest.

_____

_____

Good News:

"I will praise God with a song" (Psalm 69:30).

Quiet Time:

Thank You, God, for making me a person of promise. Help me reach my full potential.

So John went throughout the whole territory of the Jordan River,
preaching, "Turn away from your sins and be baptized, and God will
forgive your sins."
— Luke 3:3

Obedience School

▼

Tough Times:

Open your Bible to Luke 3. Verses 4–6 repeat the Old Testament
prophecy written in the book of Isaiah. Where was the voice in this
prophecy coming from? _____ Luke 3:2 tells
you that John was in the _____ when the
word of the Lord came to him.

Life in the desert must have been hard and lonely. John learned
to take care of himself. He ate simple food, probably wild honey
and locusts. He wore rough, plain robes made from animal hides.

John had been in the desert for years learning from God what
He wanted him to know. John needed this time to get ready to
preach. He needed to be ready to prepare the way for the coming
Messiah. Much of John's time was spent praying and listening to
God. John must have thought often about the Scripture he had
been taught as a young child.

John was the first prophet to come in over four hundred years.
The people had been waiting to hear this message. John had studied his lessons well while in the desert. He was now obediently pro-
claiming the message that people must change the way they were
living in order to be ready for the Messiah.

Write an advertisement about John's obedience. _____

_____

_____

_____

Staying Cool:

John's obedience school was in the desert. Your school is probably not located in a desert. It may be a large school in a big city. It may be a community school in a rural area. Where your school is located should not be that important. What you think about your school is important.

All schools have rules. What you think about the rules and how you follow them says alot about you. Think about what rules at school you find hard to obey. Are there any rules that you like? ____

Write an advertisement about your school, using some of the rules to tell about the kind of school you attend. Remember the definition for an advertisement.

_____

_____

_____

_____

How you follow the rules is an advertisement about you and an advertisement for your school.

Good News:

"The Lord is friend of those who obey him" (Psalm 30:14).

Quiet Time:

Thank You, Lord, for rules that help me know how to live. Help me respond positively to the rules that I must follow in my life.

People's hopes began to rise, and they began to wonder whether John perhaps might be the Messiah.
— Luke 3:15

Popularity

▼

Tough Times:

John's message had been heard by many people. The people were coming long distances to hear him preach. He was very popular. People believed his message and were making changes in the way they lived. Read Luke 3:15–22.

This was an exciting time for the young prophet. Remember, a prophet is someone who predicts things that will happen in the future. Sometimes the future is closer than people think.

One day when John was baptizing a group of people, he looked into the crowd and saw his cousin Jesus. When he recognized Him, John knew that He was the Messiah. Jesus came up and asked to be baptized. After Jesus' baptism His earthly ministry began. Jesus was now the One the people would follow.

John had done his job well. He had prepared the people for the coming of Jesus. Even though some still followed John, it wasn't long before John's popularity started slipping. What words in verse 16 tell you that John understood that his popularity would change?

_____

Write an advertisement about John's popularity. _____

_____

_____

Staying Cool:

Michael's team was playing for the championship of the soccer tournament. Lots of Michael's classmates had come to cheer. In the last half, the score was tied at 1.

Michael was the team's goalie. He had been playing well all season. Several times he was voted player of the game. It was amazing how his popularity had grown.

In the final minute of play the score was still tied. Michael was watching closely. He was glad the play was on the other end of the field. Suddenly someone intercepted the ball and started toward Michael. Michael readied himself. His other teammates were running hard and fast down the field. The soccer ball suddenly was kicked toward the goal. Just as Michael thought he would successfully defend his goal, a teammate dived for the ball and tipped it into the net. The referee blew his whistle to signal a score.

Shock registered on Michael's face as he heard the horn on the scoreboard sound the end of the game. He couldn't believe they had lost.

As the team climbed aboard the bus, the silence was deafening. None of his friends had waited around. "It doesn't take much for your popularity to change," Michael mumbled to himself.

Has anything happened in your life to cause your popularity to change? Tell about it here. _____

_____

Good News:

"I trust in his constant love forever and ever" (Psalm 52:8).

Quiet Time:

Lord, even though others' feelings may change, I know that I can always count on You.

_____

[John's disciples asked,] "Are you the one John said was going to come or should we expect someone else?" [Jesus said,] "How happy are those who have no doubts about me!"
— Luke 7:19,23

Doubts

Tough Times:

Read Luke 7:18–20 to find out who had doubts and what he was doubting. Look back to Luke 3:20 to find out where John was at the time he sent his two disciples to find Jesus. Where was John?

_____

People in prison probably have a lot of time on their hands. I imagine John was doing a lot of thinking about his life. John must have felt cut off from all the action. He may have even thought he was forgotten by everyone. What question did John ask his disciples to ask Jesus? _____

_____

Was John doubting Jesus? _____

Read Luke 7:21–22. What did Jesus say the men were to tell John?

_____

In verse 23 Jesus made a statement about people who doubt. What did He say? _____

Write an advertisement for Jesus from information you learned in this passage. _____
_____
_____

Staying Cool:

When you have doubts about something or someone, you cannot put your trust in that particular thing or person. John was having doubts about Jesus being the Messiah. To remove his doubts, he asked questions of Jesus.

What do you have doubts about? Are you unsure about yourself or others? Are you uncertain about the outcome of something? How do you handle your doubts? What do your doubts say about you?

Make a list of your doubts. Next to each one, tell the cause for the doubt and what you can do to change the doubt.

_____ : _____
_____
_____ : _____
_____
_____ : _____
_____
_____ : _____
_____

Good News:

"Trust in God at all times, my people. Tell him all your troubles, for he is our refuge" (Psalm 62:8).

Quiet Time:

Lord, take my doubts away and help me to be more trusting.

This made the king very sad, but he could not refuse her because of the vows he had made in front of all his guests.
— Mark 6:26

Mistakes

T o u g h   T i m e s :

Read the story of John's death found in Mark 6:14–29.

Why was John in prison? _____

_____ (verses 17–18)

Who had a grudge against John? _____(verse 19)

Why could Herodias not get John killed? _____(verse 19)

Why was Herod afraid of John? _____(verse 20)

When did Herodias get her chance? _____(verse 21)

Who danced for the king? _____(verse 22)

What did Herod do to show he was pleased? _____

_____(verse 22–23)

Who helped the girl decide? _____(verse 24)

What did the girl ask for? _____ (verse 25)

How do you know the king knew he made a mistake? _____

_____(verse 26)

Herod knew he had made a mistake, but he thought more of himself than he did of saving John's life. Write an advertisement about Herod and his mistake. _____

_____

_____

_____

Staying Cool:

Too often, protecting your own reputation is more important than owning up to or accepting responsibility for your mistakes. How can you correct a mistake if you don't admit that you have made it? Today tell about a time when you made a mistake? What did you do when you realized it was a mistake. What did you learn from the mistake? What did you learn about yourself?

_____

_____

_____

_____

_____

_____

_____

_____

Good News:

"Keep me from going the wrong way, and in your goodness teach me your law" (Psalm 119:29).

Quiet Time:

Sometime, I make mistakes because I don't think about the actions I take. I am often embarrassed by them. Help me, Lord, know how to handle my mistakes so that I may be a good advertisement.

"For John is the one of whom the scripture says: 'God said, I will send my messenger ahead of you to open the way for you.' I tell you," Jesus added, "John is greater than any man who has ever lived."
— Luke 7:27–28

Praise

▼

T o u g h   T i m e s :

Open your Bible to Luke 7:24–28. Read the passage to find out who spoke the words of praise for John.

Who praised John? _____

Who heard the words of praise? _____

Words of praise are used to show high regard or approval. In this passage what words did Jesus use that let you know He was praising John? _____

_____

The people listened to Jesus' words of praise.

How often do you use words of praise? Do you find it easy to praise people when they do things well? Do you find it hard to praise a friend for being a winner? How does praise make you feel?

In the space below, write an advertisement using words of praise to describe God. _____

_____

_____

Staying Cool:

Remember, you placed a picture of your family in the chapter's introduction. Today think about how you are a part of God's family. Either draw a picture or design a "Graffiti Wall" using names of people that have been a good advertisement for God in your life. Next to each picture or name, tell how that person has influenced your belief about God.

Good News:

"Help me to speak, Lord, and I will praise you" (Psalm 51:15).

Quiet Time:

Help me, Lord, use only words that praise Your name and make me a good advertisement for You.

Chapter Twelve

Cool Living

▼

Cool living is excellent, or first-rate, living. Do you believe that? Do you know what the keys to cool living are?

For you to remain "cool" in all of life's situations, you must first turn your life over to God. This chapter will help you know how to become one of God's children. Then you will explore what Paul has to say in Romans 12–13 about living a life committed to Christ—"cool living."

Look at the list of words and statements below. With your highlighter mark each word that describes you and the way you live your life.

Seek God's will	Saved	Different
Self-giving	Pray	Disciple
Worshiper of God	Loving	Study the Bible
Do good	Peacemaker	Put others first
Obey God's laws	Honest	A witness

Look over Romans 12 and 13 to see if you can find other words to add to the list that describe cool living.

Chapter's Challenge:

To know and accept God and His will for my life of "cool" Christian living.

"Repent, then, and turn to God so that he will forgive your sins."
— Acts 3:19

Salvation Is the Beginning

▼

Tough Times:

What is *salvation*? Salvation is the saving of a life from death or harm. In the New Testament, salvation means to deliver one from the penalty and power of sin. When sin controls your life, you cannot be living a godly life.

The following list of Scriptures will help you know how to receive God's gift of salvation. Look up each verse, and then match the verse with what it is telling you to do.

Romans 3:23	You must believe
Romans 6:23	You must repent
John 3:16	You must confess
Romans 5:8–10	You are a sinner
Acts 3:19	God's gift
Ephesians 2:8	Penalty for sin
Romans 10:9–10	Accept by faith
Romans 10:13	Christ paid penalty

The verses are in the right order. Now put the answers in the right order. The order is important because you must follow these steps in this order to become a Christian. A Christian is someone who has accepted Christ's free gift of salvation.

Staying Cool:

If you have not accepted Christ as your personal Savior, use the information on the preceding page as you talk to a parent or other adult. Let them answer your questions about what you need to do to become a Christian.

If you have already accepted Christ as your personal Savior, you are a Christian. Use this space to tell about your salvation experience. Include in your salvation story the difference Christ makes in your life today.

_____

_____

_____

_____

_____

_____

_____

_____

_____

_____

Good News:

"For God loved the world so much that he gave his only Son, so that everyone who believes in him may not die but have eternal life" (John 3:16).

Quiet Time:

If you do not know the passage above, learn it. Write a prayer asking God's forgiveness of your sins. Tell Him how much you love Him and want Him to be in control of your life.

Do not conform yourselves to the standards of this world.
— Romans 12:2

Must Be Different!

▼

Tough Times:

Read Romans 12:1–2. With a highlighter, mark all the bold phrases (below) in your Bible that tell you how a Christian is different.

Living sacrifice. When you are a "living sacrifice," you are living as God wants you to live. You are totally committed to God. What does total commitment mean to you? _____

_____

Dedicated to His service. *Dedicate* means to set apart or present for a special purpose or use. Tell how your life shows it has a special purpose. _____

Pleasing to Him means the way you live is acceptable to God. Are the things you do acceptable to God? _____

"Do not conform yourself to the standards of this world." Whose standards should you follow if you obey this verse ? _____

_____

The last phrase is **"Let God transform you inwardly by a complete change of your mind."** The word *transform* means change. When you let God have control, He will change the way you think. Has God transformed you? What would be different about the way you live if God changed you? _____

_____

You have to live in this world, but this verse tells you that you should not live by this world's standards. Knowing God's will and doing it is what makes the Christian different.

Staying Cool:

You may have trouble thinking about being different because acceptance is very important to you. Below is a list of how God expects you to live. Next to each statement tell if you follow or don't follow God's expectations.

- Keep the Sabbath holy._____
- Do not use the Lord's name in a wrong way. _____
- Honor your parents._____
- Do not murder. _____
- Do not steal. _____
- Do not lie. _____
- Do not falsely accuse._____
- Do not want what belongs to another. _____

Read God's standards in Exodus 20:3–17, the Ten Commandments.

Good News:

"Do not conform yourselves to the standards of this world, but let God transform you inwardly by a complete change of your mind" (Romans 12:2).

Quiet Time:

Help me, Lord, to live by Your standards so that my life can be a witness for You.

Love must be completely sincere. Hate what is evil and hold on to what is good. Love one another warmly as Christian brothers, and be eager to show respect for one another.
— Romans 12:9–10

Love and Respect

▼

Tough Times:

Define *love.* _____

In today's world the word *love* is used to describe one's feelings about all kinds of things. Think about how often you use the word love to describe your feelings? What do you mean when you use the word love?_____

_____

Open your Bible and read Romans 12:9–13. The love described in this passage is sacrificial, self-giving love—the kind of love that wants only the best for the other person. This kind of love hates evil and looks for the good.

Verse 10 talks about "brotherly love," when it says that you should love one another as Christian brothers. This same verse also talks about respect. Respect is a high regard, favorable opinion, or admiration for another person. To whom does this verse say you should show respect?_____

What place does sacrificial, self-giving love have in your life? _____

_____

Are you willing to put others first? Does the amount of respect you show reflect your real feelings?_____

Staying Cool:

Can you "live cool" and still have an attitude of love and respect? The way you choose to live your life reflects what you really believe. Tell how you demonstrate an attitude of love and respect in the following situations:

• Toward your parents _____

_____

• Toward your brothers and/or sisters _____

_____

• Toward your teachers _____

_____

• Toward your friends _____

_____

• At church _____

_____

• At the mall _____

_____

• At school _____

_____

• On a sports team _____

_____

• About your homework _____

_____

• About your responsibilities at home _____

_____

Good News:

"Love one another warmly as Christian brothers, and be eager to show respect for one another" (Romans 12:10).

Quiet Time:

Lord, may my attitude and actions reflect my true feelings of love and respect toward others.

Do not let evil defeat you; instead, conquer evil with good.
— Romans 12:21

Good over Evil

▼

Tough Times:

"Cool living" requires one to always work for peace. Have you ever observed "hot heads" in action? Stop and think what happens when they "lose their cool."

Open your Bible to Romans 12 and read verses 17–21. Define each of the following words from the passage by looking up each word in your dictionary; then write a definition that reflects "cool living."

• Good: _____

• Wrong:_____

• Peace:_____

• Revenge: _____

• Anger: _____

• Pay back: _____

• Enemy: _____

• Shame:_____

• Defeat:_____

• Evil: _____

• Conquer: _____

Is it possible for you to do what this passage says?_____
Verse 19 says that you are never to take revenge, but you are to let
God's anger do it. Tell what you think this means. _____

_____

_____

Staying Cool:

Have you ever heard the expression "kill them with kindness"? Tell
what you think that means. _____

_____

_____

If you are always seeking ways to overcome evil with good, then are
you trying to be a peacemaker. Use the space below to draw a modern-day picture which shows what this passage is saying.

_____

_____

_____

_____

_____

_____

_____

Good News:

"Do everything possible on your part to live in peace with everybody" (Romans 12:18).

Quiet Time:

Lord, I find it hard to not want to get even with those that treat me
wrong. Help me to remember Your words in this passage.

If you love someone you will never do him wrong; to love then is to obey the whole Law.
— Romans 13:10

Love Conquers All
▼

Tough Times:

Read Romans 13:8–10. Did you notice that verses 8 and 10 say almost the same thing? Paul's theme in these verses is "love one another." You have already seen those words in Romans 12:10.

Think about love as your duty or obligation. Look closely at verse 8. What does this verse mean? _____

_____

Verse 9 refers once again to some of the Ten Commandments. Which commandments does this verse mention? _____

_____

Verse 9 ends with a summary statement about love. Write the statement. _____

_____

Think about how different this world would be if people would love their neighbors and do for them whatever they would do for themselves. Who is your neighbor? Is it possible for you to carry out this modern-day commandment of showing love to everyone?

_____

_____

The last part of verses 8 and 10 refers to the Law. God's Law is one of love toward everyone. When you love everyone you will do no one _____ (verse 10), and this kind of love is a way of obeying the _____ (verse 10).

As a Christian you must live in this world. You can take a positive approach to life. Isn't that what these verses are asking you to do?

Staying Cool:
Think about the positive effect love can have on this world. Think of a current event or something that has happened recently that demonstrates that "love conquers all." Share your information below by telling it as if you were telling a story to your best friend.

_____

_____

_____

_____

_____

_____

_____

_____

Good News:
"'Love the Lord your God with all your heart, with all your soul, and with all your mind.' This is the greatest and the most important commandment. The second most important commandment is like it: 'Love your neighbor as you love yourself'" (Matthew 22:37–39).

Quiet Time:
Lord, may love be the powerful force in my life that helps me be a positive witness of Your love.

Let us conduct ourselves properly, as people who live in the light of day.
— Romans 13:13

Living in the Light

▼

Tough Times:

On the lines below write as many adjectives as you can think of that describe your world. _____

_____

_____

Did you use the word *sinful?*_____

Open your Bible and read Romans 13:11–14. What kinds of behavior did Paul warn against in verse 13b?_____

_____

_____

Do you see or hear about these kinds of behavior today?_____

These verses could be a warning to people today. In verse 11 Paul said it's time for the people to wake up. In verse 12 Paul showed the difference between sinfulness and righteousness when he used the words *night* and *day* and *dark* and *light*. The words *night* and *dark* refer to sinfulness, and *day* and *light* refer to God's righteousness (goodness).

Verse 14 is a command to take up the weapons of the _____.
Weapons does not mean guns. This verse means to be like Christ so
that you can be His witness in this world.

If you are only trying to satisfy your selfish desires, then you
will not be Christ's witness to this world.

Staying Cool:

Romans 13:13 says that you should conduct yourself properly.
Orgies, drunkenness, immorality, indecency, fighting, and jealousy
are the kinds of conduct Paul said every Christian should avoid.

Use the space below to tell a friend about "proper Christian
conduct." Remember, as a Christian your life is a witness of this
Christian conduct.

_____

_____

_____

_____

_____

_____

_____

_____

Good News:

"Let us conduct ourselves properly, as people who live in the light
of day" (Romans 13:13).

Quiet Time:

Lord, as one of Your children, may the way I live my life show that
I truly believe You are coming again.

So then, my brothers, because of God's great mercy to us I appeal to you: Offer yourselves as a living sacrifice to God, dedicated to his service and pleasing to him. This is the true worship that you should offer.
— Romans 12:1

Key to Cool Living

▼

T o u g h   T i m e s :

This last session will challenge you to look closely at how you can be a "living sacrifice."

Sacrifice is defined as an offering to a god or the giving up of something for the sake of something else.

Romans 12:1 tells you why you should be a living sacrifice. First, "because of God's great mercy" means that because God has shown you great love and goodness, you should live your life in a manner that is acceptable to God.

Second, when you "dedicate" your life to God, you should be willing to serve Him. Your service should be pleasing. Your service (actions) indicates your true feelings of love for God.

Giving yourself to God is an act of "true worship." Worship is a way of living out your belief or faith in God. Is the way you live a sacrifice? Tell how the way you live is a "living sacrifice" and witness to your world. _____

_____

_____

Staying Cool:

Your key to "cool living" is following God. Most of the problems that you will encounter in trying to live the Christian life will come from trying to only "half live it." This means you are still trying to live by two standards—God's and the world's depending on which is the most convenient at the time.

The things listed below will help you live for God. Take a few minutes to think about the part each one plays in your life. What keeps you from doing any of them?

Praying   Telling others
Bible study   Attending worship services
Loving everyone   Sharing the good news about Jesus
Living a godly life   Seeking God's will

Usually you are influenced to follow the ways of the world by someone that has become more important in your life than God. Read the following saying several times each day for the next week. Then you will know how to respond when someone tries to persuade you *not* to follow God's way.

"I am a Christian.
I won't do _____.(Name the things you won't do)
I'm cool.
I live for God."

Good News:

"Now that you know the truth, how happy you will be if you put it into practice!" (John 13:17)

Quiet Time:

Lord, the next time I'm faced with a decision about how I should live, help me remember that "cool living" requires my total commitment to You and Your will for my life.